A Tale of Two Nations: Canada, U.S. and WWI

A Tale of Two Nations, Volume 6

Melina Druga

Published by Sun Up Press, 2021.

Table of Contents

"Royal Couple Slain by Assassin" 1
"War Call Comes" 5
"Europe's War Cloud Darkens" 9
"Canada Will Back Britain" 15
Ypres: Baptism of Fire and Blood 23
Saving Those Who Could Be Saved 31
Lusitania: Hubris Unsinkable 35
War Temperature Rises 45
He's Our Man 53
The Bloodiest Day 65
A Glorious Victory, But At What Cost? 67
Too Close to Call 73
The Climate Changes 79
Succeed Where Others Could Not 91
Peace at Last 97
A Time to Die 103
Glossary 109
Sources 111

Sun Up Press

All rights reserved. No part of this publication may be reproduced, distributed, or transmitted in any form or by any means, including photocopying, recording, scanning, or other electronic or mechanical methods, without the prior written permission of the publisher, except in the case of brief quotations embodied in critical reviews and certain other noncommercial uses permitted by copyright law.

This book is a work of fiction. Names, characters, places, and incidents either are the product of the author's imagination, or are used fictitiously. Any resemblance to actual persons, living or dead, events, or locales is entirely coincidental.

The eBook version of this book is not to be copied, shared or resold. Downloading pirated eBooks is a crime. Neither authors nor publishers receive payment from pirated books.

Copyright 2018 by Melina Druga

Melina Druga

www.melinadruga.com

Editor: John Druga

Cover art: Sun Up Press.

EBook cover image: The remains of the Hotel de Ville at Arras

Introduction

World War I, like most wars, was started by politicians and fought by ordinary men who generally had no stake in the conflict. They fought because of patriotic fervor or a sense of adventure, and millions lost their lives as a consequence.

Between 1914 and 1918, nearly 5 million Americans and Canadians served in the war. While today the two neighboring nations share a sense of common heritage, language, history and cooperation, in the 1910s there was a lingering sense of animosity.

The Canada of 1914 was much different from the Canada of today. It was less than 50 years old, founded primarily by English and French decedents, and had been the refuge of Loyalists during and after the American Revolution. It was a dominion of the British Empire, autonomous when it came to everything but foreign affairs. Its population during the 1911 census was 7.2 million, not much larger than the population of Greater Toronto 100 years later.

The United States had a population 13 times larger, at 92.2 million strong, and played a greater role on the world stage. Many in the U.S. felt Canada should be part of the union, as a natural extension of Manifest Destiny, and countless Canadians feared annexation. Immediately following the American Civil War, the Fenian Brotherhood, Irishmen who had served in the Union Army, conducted raids into Southern Canada in the hopes of agitating Great Britain. A few years later, Canada had an interest in purchasing Alaska, but negotiations favored the Americans. The final blow was the attempt to establish a trade reciprocity agreement between the U.S. and Canada. Congress rejected the agreement on multiple occasions and, in the 1911 election, so did the Canadian electorate.

On the eve of the Great War, newspapers in both the U.S. and Canada were filled with news of the upcoming conflict; the great European powers were at each other's throats, figuratively and perhaps soon literally. How each nation viewed the war, however, betrayed its interests and shaped public opinion.

A Tale of Two Nations is the story of North American countries that found themselves embroiled in an European war – one by circumstance and one by choice. It discusses two pivotal events from each year of the Great War – one from an American perspective and one from a Canadian one – and reveals how newspapers at the time handled wartime coverage.

A Tale of Two Nations does not look at the First World War with the benefit of hindsight and analysis. Instead, it uses contemporary newspaper reports that often were inaccurate, incomplete or even chaotic. Wartime censorship and bias also played a role.

It is as much the story of journalism as it is the story of World War I. In the early 20th century, the newspaper was king. Many towns and cities had multiple papers, and it was common for larger papers to print multiple editions. Most articles had no bylines, and publications filled their pages with as much news as possible, with some news briefs being as short as a sentence or two.

In Part one, 1914, the war begins. Canada is proud to contribute to the war effort while the United States declares its neutrality.

In Part two, spring 1915 is consumed with two traumatic events. The Canadian Expeditionary Force passes its trial by fire, entering battle for the first time and winning glory while becoming victims of a chlorine gas attack. A month later, the United States is shocked that German submarine warfare has killed civilians. The *Lusitania* is sunk, and war rhetoric is on the rise.

In Part three, 1916, Canada participates in the Battle of the Somme, one of the bloodiest battles in history and the battle that introduces the tank, yet papers back home are preoccupied elsewhere. In the United States, the presidential election of 1916 brings out opposing viewpoints. Will the populous re-elect President Woodrow Wilson who kept the nation out of the war, or will the electorate go in a different direction?

In Part four, 1917, the Battle of Vimy Ridge often is called Canada's coming of age, but is that how contemporary newspapers viewed the victory? Meanwhile, not long after his second inauguration, President Woodrow Wilson, following years of pledging American neutrality, declares war on Germany.

In Part five, 1918, Armistice is declared at last, ending the Great War. However, joy is tempered by the Spanish Flu pandemic.

Part 1: 1914

"Royal Couple Slain by Assassin"

Imagine you have access to a time machine. You travel to various locations in June 1914 and stop at newsstands to see what locals are discussing. Newspapers in Canada and the United States are full of ads hoping to snag the tired city slicker looking for adventure. You could travel from New York City to Niagara Falls for $10, and Montrealers could trek to the Atlantic shore for as little as $12. Retailers also hope to take advantage of pleasure seekers. Summer sales promote the advantages of buying new swimsuits and light dresses.

There's riveting news, as well, interspersed among the usual crime reports, society pages and car accident stories. Manitoba is in the midst of a political crisis, the American Southwest is obsessed with Pancho Villa's exploits during the Mexican Revolution, and plague has been diagnosed in New Orleans, causing concern in the city and surrounding areas.

When people in North America rose on the morning of June 27, nobody knew it would be the last day of peace, the final day before the lives of millions globally would be shattered first by world war and then by the Spanish Flu pandemic.

That day the *New York Times* reported on the formal grand opening of the Kaiser Wilhelm Canal in Germany, which was larger than the Panama Canal and better able to respond to shipping demands. The official reason was an increase in commerce, but military operations, the paper said, necessitated the expansion as dreadnoughts had grown in size.

"In 1912 there were 1,400 passages of German warships through the canal," the *Times* said. "The vessels included nine battleships. These figures show the value of the canal to the German Navy in times of peace."

A peace that was not to last.

While traveling through Sarajevo, Bosnia, on June 28, the heir to the Austrian-Hungarian Empire, Archduke Franz Ferdinand, and his wife Sophie were shot and killed by Slavic nationalist Gavrilo Princip. The shooting had been the second attempt on their lives that day. Earlier, an explosive lobbed at their car had been deflected and exploded beneath another vehicle, injuring the occupants.

The couple was on their way to visit the wounded in the hospital when Princip struck. Duchess Sophie initially was frightened to be traveling again in an open car. Bosnia's Governor Potiorek persuaded her otherwise.

"It's all over," he told the couple. "We have not more than one murderer in the city."

"Franz Joseph Made Saddest Monarch of Europe by Successive Tragedies"

Austro-Hungarian Emperor Franz Joseph was swamped with grief upon learning of his nephew and heir apparent's death.

"His [Franz Joseph's] reign has been a succession of defeats, disappointments, domestic troubles, deaths, assassinations, intrigues, and disgrace," the *Chicago Tribune* reported. "He was beaten in battle after battle, flung out of kingdom after kingdom, tricked successfully by Frenchman, ItaMan [sic] and German.

"He never won a great battle; he failed repeatedly at diplomacy; he fired on his own capital; he was forced to ruthlessly suppress half his subjects; he was forced to beg for alms from Russia and to yield to the Magyars."

The reason for all this sadness was clear, according the *Tribune* anyway. The emperor and his deceased nephew were members of the Hapsburg family, and the Hapsburgs had been cursed since 1848 by words spoken "with all the hatred and vindictiveness of a woman whose heart was torn by grief."

The idea of a curse sounds ridiculous to modern readers, but then again, considering the elderly emperor did ultimately lose the war and the Austrian-Hungarian Empire crumbled, perhaps there is some validly to it.

"Wife Blamed for His Act"

It wasn't immediately clear that the assassination would lead to war, although civil unrest and riots erupted in the Balkans after the couple's death. Franz Ferdinand wasn't well liked. It began when he married Sophie, a lady in waiting, someone considered to be of a lower social class. He loved her and insisted on marrying her, despite the objections of many. The marriage was permitted under the condition that, once he became emperor, he never elevated his wife or children to the position of imperial rank.

Everything might had been forgiven if Sophie had been liked, but she wasn't. She was described as an ambitious woman who was not content with staying in the background as a demure consort.

"The manner in which she pushed herself forward, her lack of tact and of distinction, her constant quarrels and fights for precedence," the *Chicago Tribune* said, "her fits of anger at what she considered to be an act of deference to her rank, had the consequence of embittering all the imperial family against her, and, incidentally against her husband, who became wholly alienated from his imperial relatives."

The archduke had been given power over the years he was never intended to have because of Franz Joseph's illnesses. This made the archduke involve himself in politics and become a "disturbing factor" on the world stage.

Sophie's influence was blamed for both her husband's politics and the couple's death. "Her death under such shocking circumstances serves once more as warning to those women who aspire to imperial and royal honors to which they have not been born," the Tribune said.

"Reports to Capital Ominous"

American diplomats in several European capitals were instructed to notify Washington immediately of any developments in the "European situation." In the days following the assassination, reports spoke of an impending war.

By July, European negotiations to avoid war were failing, and soon the following dispatch appeared in North American newspapers:

"The royal government not having replied in a satisfactory manner to the note remitted to it by the Austro-Hungarian minister in Belgrade on July 23, 1914, the imperial and royal government finds itself compelled to proceed itself to safeguard its rights and interests and to have recourse for this purpose to force arms.

"Austria-Hungary considers itself therefore from this moment in a state of war with Servia [sic]."

In Canada, there was hope the war would not spread to Britain and its empire. "Diplomats in London," the *Winnipeg Tribune* reported, "while they confess the situation is most grave, believe there is hope of averting a conflict."

These hopes hinged on Austria-Hungary holding what the paper called "conversations" with Russia. Russia was treaty bound to come to Serbia's aid, and war with Serbia meant war with Russia. The Germans, meanwhile, were bound to come to Austria-Hungary's aid in conflicts.

While Canadian papers fretted about the war, American publications reported on President Woodrow Wilson's upcoming vacation to his summer home. "The President has been bearing up well under the hot weather of the last few weeks," the Associated Press said, "but he is anxious to get Mrs. Wilson away from Washington."

Once summer break was over, Wilson planned to help Democratic candidates with their election campaigns.

Life, in the United States anyway, was continuing as if the assassination never happened.

"War Call Comes"

As President Wilson was preparing for his vacation, American and Canadian tourists in Europe were altering their travel plans.

In Paris, thousands of Americans flocked to the U.S. consulate. They weren't panicked, but they wanted to know how long they could stay in the City of Lights without jeopardizing their return home. Americans called the U.S. consulate and embassy to ask not only this but if it was safe to travel into Austria and Germany. Phone calls increased from an average of 60 a day to 700.

Diplomats could not give specific answers and only could advise that if war spread into France, the chances of getting home were slim.

Many, however, refused to let anything spoil their fun. Large numbers of Americans were traveling overseas despite rumors of war, and as a London hotel manager said, "Our American guests are not easily induced to give up their plans."

One tourist agency manager told the *New York Times*, "There has been no noticeable let up in the rush to France, German and Switzerland. We are also selling many tickets to Austria today, despite the printed dispatches from Vienna that the railways have been taken over by the military and traffic for the general public is suspended. Many travelers, mostly Americans, are willing to take the chance of getting into Austria and out again."

The English were postponing their trips, the manager said, but Americans refused.

Canadian tourists were not as reckless as the Americans. They cancelled trips. Canadian Pacific Railroad, which also operated ships, found that most of its passengers were now military men seeking transport to England.

By July 31, the U.S. government had begun warning tourists not to travel abroad or else they risked being marooned in Europe until the war's end.

"If Armageddon Comes"

It didn't take long for American tourists to begin purchasing passports at the embassies and consulates. Most tourists didn't have one, viewing them as unnecessary, but with "war drums beating along the Danube" they gladly paid the $2.

"Nine out of ten are now busily figuring what steamers will safely carry them home," the *New York Times* said. "They know it is the business of warships not only to destroy an enemy's warships, but also to capture or sink passenger ships. They are occupied, therefore, with trying to figure out on what route the peril is the least."

Nevertheless, the "spectacle" of a nation preparing for war thrilled tourists who were waiting on travel news in Berlin. And Berlin hotels appreciated the business.

While American newspapers reported on the tourists' calmness and disregard for current events, Canadian reports told a different story.

"The American tourists who are endeavoring to return home are in a panicky condition," the *Winnipeg Tribune* said.

Tourists in Antwerp were so desperate to gain passage on a streamer traveling to the United States that they left their luggage behind, the *Tribune* said.

It wasn't just tourists who feared becoming trapped on the Continent. Around 18,000 Canadian men working in the shipping industry were in Europe. "No means has yet been devised to bring them home again," the *Tribune* said.

"Lives and Money Offered in Defense of Native Land"

Tourists and merchant marines weren't the only ones who had the potential to be stuck abroad. Foreign nationals in the U.S. and Canada were itching to get back to Europe and fight for their birth nations.

The Austrian-Hungarian consulate in Winnipeg telegraphed 12,000 Austrians living in the city and told them to mobilize as reservists. The empire also was expected to call the 280,000 Ruthenians [an ethnic group that includes Eastern Slavs like Lithuanians and Belarussians] living in Western Canada. The *Winnipeg Tribune* reported leaders of this group had nothing to gain from mobilization and were happy to remain in Canada.

In Chicago, 1,500 "warlike" Serbs rallied at a meeting, calling "Down with Austria" and wearing badges reading "To hell with Austria."

"Are you cowards, you men who hear me," one of the speakers said, "or will you come across the sea with me and give up your lives for the country of your forefathers?"

All the men responded with an enthusiastic "yes."

In Vancouver and Victoria, Germans were being called home to serve the Fatherland. Local German newspapers, however, were urging nationalized Germans to stay in Canada and fight for their adopted country.

Similarly, Swiss citizens were ordered home by the consulate to join the mobilizing Swiss Army.

"Neutrality Puzzle"

By August, the efforts of foreign nations to recall their citizens had attracted the attention of the U.S. government, which was concerned that ads placed in several major newspapers violated neutrality laws.

Enlistment was forbidden under the laws and so was the departure of war vessels from the U.S. that were hostile to U.S.-friendly countries. Foreigners were permitted to leave on their own accord. It was when their movements were directed by other nations, or they were provided help with expenses, that the government feared the laws were violated.

This concern came with some past experience. During the Crimean War, British Minister Sir John Fiennes Twisleton Crampton tried to recruit Americans. Interested men were directed from consulates in three U.S. cities to Halifax where they enlisted in the British Army. Once the U.S. government discovered Crampton's actions, he was forced to resign his position as the top British diplomat in the U.S.

"Europe's War Cloud Darkens"

On Aug. 1, France declared that war was mere hours away. A last ditch effort was made to negotiate a way out of a global conflict. Britain and France hoped Germany and Austria-Hungary would agree to a deal that would be beneficial to both them and Russia.

The Russian foreign minister and the German ambassador met in Paris for the negotiations.

German Count Friedrich von Pourtales asked if Russia would demobilize under the condition that Austria would not keep any Serbian land. Russian Foreign Minister Sergius Sazonoff replied this was not enough and that Russia could not allow the extermination of Serbia by Austria.

When asked what would make Russia demobilize, Sazonoff was adamant that Austria was the aggressor, having committed an act of war, and that only Austria would answer this question.

The negotiations went no further.

The following evening, Germany declared war on Russia.

An editorial in the *Winnipeg Tribune* blamed the war on radicalism and resentment. The assassination of the archduke and his wife was the flame that ignited the resentment and had the militarist powers of the world poised for war.

"The student who did the deed at Sarajevo, Bosnia," the editorial said, "on June 25th last, probably considered in the enthusiasm of youth, that he was actuated by the loftiest spirit of racial loyalty and patriotism. He was inspired, it is evidently believed in Austria, by leaders of the Pan-Servian movement in Belgrade, Servia, and hence this peremptory demand of Austria for an apology and the punishment of these Servian agitators."

"End of the World"

An editorial published in the religion section of the *Chicago Tribune* on Aug. 2 posed an interesting question: Is this the end of the world as prophesied by St. John?

"Is a universal conflagration in Europe – a conflict between a triple alliance [Germany, Austria-Hungary and Italy] and the triple entente [the United Kingdom, France and Russia] – to be the fulfillment of the prophesy of St. John?" the editorial began.

"Or–" it went on to say, "is it merely one of the great international conflicts, one of the historical events of tremendous economic and social importance, which Mme. Thebes, the famous seeress [sic] of Paris, declared would come to pass in 1914?"

The editorial also quoted several passages from the book of Revelation before speaking again of Mme. Thebes, who appeared to be a female Nostradamus. She predicted, among other events, the Paris Bazaar Fire of 1897, the 1906 San Francisco earthquake and the Balkan Wars.

Thebes was quoted as having said, "France will be drawn into war. An era of love, peace, great hopes and great labors will date from the end of 1914. But first the waves must be tinted with blood, and water and fire must combat in subterranean forces. Signs will appear in the sky. French troops will rush for the frontier. The German emperor will come to Paris, but not as a king!"

The *Tribune* also reported that the author Leo Tolstoy had predicted a European war in 1910. The author said he had a vision on more than one occasion of a beautiful, naked woman named Commercialism. She held three torches. The first torch was the flame of war. The second torch was bigotry and hypocrisy while the third torch was the law. By 1915, Tolstoy said, all of Europe would be in flames.

"Russo-German War"

The first shots of the conflict reported in Canadian and American newspapers referred to the impending world war as the Russo-German war. Shots were fired outside the town of Prostken in East Prussia. The Russians fired first on the Germans who returned fire. There were no causalities.

Meanwhile, Britain announced it had built a new dreadnaught, the Queen Mary, for $10.1 million. This would be the nation's 18th dreadnaught-class ship. Each had the capacity of traveling more than 28 knots an hour and each carried 10 1.35 caliber guns.

Should Britain join the Triple Entente, the battleship would be put into service, possibly in a blockade of Germany and Austria-Hungary. This was deemed essential war work as Germany annually imported $1.5 billion more in food and agricultural products than it exported.

"The British navy strangled Napoleon," the *Chicago Tribune* said. "Will it strangle Germany?"

"Latest Figures in Armies"

"If the entire strength of the nations involved were placed in the field – or if a fair proportion of them were called out – they would make the armies of past conflicts seem small by comparison," the *Winnipeg Tribune* said Aug. 3.

Serbia had a war strength of 240,000 men, and its ally Russia 5 million more. Globally, 34 million men were available to fight.

Great Britain had the largest navy available with 569 battleships and submarines.

German had the largest available reserve of aircraft, 350 airplanes and seaplanes, more than the number of Britain's available pilots.

The members of the Triple Alliance had a population totaling 149.9 million while the Triple Entente had a population of 272.5 million. The Triple Entente also outnumbered the Triple Alliance in terms of geographic territory, army men and reservists, battleships and aircraft.

"To Add One Billion Dollars"

While Europeans and resident foreigners were fearful war was imminent, American economists saw it as an opportunity. "War in Europe means prosperity in the United States," a federal agent said.

War would be a boon for merchants and manufacturers, both of which would benefit from double the exports, and ships would easily enter European ports while flying a neutral flag.

Unlike elsewhere in the world, the New York Stock Exchange was thriving. Most of the other stock exchanges in North America and Europe had suspended operations, but on July 29 alone 800,000 shares were aggregated globally. Of those, 25,000 shares were aggregated at the Berlin Stock Exchange. The next day 1.3 million shares were sold.

"Canadian Pacific," the *Chicago Tribune* said, "the source of great weakness recently, and a prime Berlin favorite, was taken in large amounts at almost uninterrupted advances. The German capital also bought extensively of other American shares, while Paris and London continue to unload here."

The *Tribune* cautioned, however, that war would bring higher food prices as war would destroy European crops and would force American farms to compensate. While U.S. farmers would benefit, the average person would find his pocketbook strained by the increased costs. A short war would be good for business, but it would be followed by a depression, economists said.

"America has everything to lose and nothing to gain if continental Europe is plunged into a prolonged war," the *Tribune* said.

"America has Billions to Meet Emergency"

To protect America's interests, the Wilson administration issued $500 million in emergency currency. "Europe mobilizes armies; we mobilize bank reserves," one government official told AP.

Billions of dollars in currency were added by an act of Congress that modified the bank laws. Before the modification, banks could issue up to $500 million; modification removed the restriction. Problem was, the currency had not been printed yet and was not in circulation.

With war on the horizon, the government also restricted money orders.

"It is the intention of the department," Postmaster-General Burleson told the Associated Press, "to so restrict the service that money cannot be transferred to Europe for speculative reasons."

War in Europe was seen as an event that needed to be exploited.

"Our country has the greatest opening in its history for expanding its foreign trade and its home industries," was the opinion of the *Los Angeles Times*.

The *Times* listed the U.S. industries that would benefit from a war in Europe. They were agriculture, food canneries, fabric mills, oil, and munitions. Increasing production in these industries would bring the U.S. $300 million annually in trade, the newspaper said.

"Get busy! Do things!" the *Times* urged.

"War Will Aid Exposition"

American tourists spent $125 million annually abroad in the years before the war. Where were these tourists to go now that Europe was torn by bloodshed? To the Pacific Coast, according to the *Times*, and recreation and exhibit halls there would gain financially from war.

Frank Wiggins, secretary for the LA Chamber of Commerce, told the *Times*, "What the majority of travelers are doing, will be done by those forced to stay in America on account of the troubles abroad."

"Canada Will Back Britain"

"If Great Britain is drawn into war, Canada will back her up to the full extent," the *Winnipeg Tribune* said July 31.

The minister of the Canadian militia, Col. Sam Hughes, held an emergency meeting. It was decided that if called, Canada would produce a first contingent consisting of 20,000 to 30,000 soldiers within two to three weeks. The small permanent force was ordered to begin preparations for mobilization, and a garrison was recalled back to its barracks in Halifax as a precaution.

The militia council was confident that within a month 100,000 men could be recruited. Active militia totaled 50,000 and with the reserve the military would reach 250,000 men.

On Aug. 1, AP reported Canada had cabled Britain's government and made a formal offer of military assistance. The offer included artillery, cavalry and infantry in the numbers quoted by the militia.

Canada also was trying to prevent Austro-Hungarian reservists from leaving the country.

"Canada's Duty"

The Canadian Press was clear on the nation's duty should Great Britain declare war.

"Canada's place is at the side of the Mother Land," the *Calgary Albertan* said. The *Calgary Herald*, the *Hamilton Times*, the *Montreal Mail* and others echoed this sentiment.

The *Hamilton Herald* and *Toronto Mail* reminded readers that when Britain is at war so is Canada. Therefore, any soldier that might ultimately be sent to the front is fighting on behalf of the defense of Canada.

Canadian newspapers in the 1910s were divided by party lines – Conservative and Liberal – and not all supported compulsory service. They felt that should war come, Canada's first move should be to defend itself. "... it is clearly the duty of the Dominion government to mobilize in the vicinity of Halifax and Quebec a large enough force to beat off landing parties from small hostile squadrons," the *Toronto Globe* said.

The *Globe* went on to say that Canada's first duty was to prevent enemy invasion and should only come to the aid of Britain in Europe if Britain were on the verge of failure.

In Halifax, preparations were underway that last occurred during the War of 1812. The port was placed under naval law, and a cruiser placed outside the harbor to direct ships to a location where they would be searched. The eastern passage to the port was blocked by a sunken schooner. Ships trying to enter the eastern passage would be fired on by the navy.

A TALE OF TWO NATIONS: CANADA, U.S. AND WWI

"Thousands [of] Canadians Volunteer"

Germany planned to quickly conquer Paris by marching through Belgium. Germany formally requested passage, but Belgium refused. Germany would not take "no" for an answer and invaded Belgium on Aug. 4. The invasion through Belgium slowed the Germans enough that, during the First Battle of Marne, Paris was saved. In what is called the Rape of Belgium, Germany occupied 95 percent of the nation, and there were 267,000 casualties. The invasion would cause Belgium's King Albert I to declare, "Belgium is a nation, not a road."

In support of Belgium sovereignty, Britain declared war on Germany. Canadians had been expecting the official declaration and waited outside newspaper offices for the war bulletin. When the news was posted, the crowds sang patriotic songs, waved flags and celebrated in the streets. . They were firm in their belief that going to war against German was just.

Newspapers seemed to be more realistic than the general populous. "The time of trial for the British Empire has arrived," the *Ottawa Journal*'s evening edition said. "This war is an unspeakable crime on the part of those who have forced it on."

Parliament had yet to decide what form mobilization should take, but it was thought enlistment would total 20,000. This would force Parliament to address the issue in a bipartisan fashion, something Canada's two parties had difficulty with in recent years.

Canadians flocked to enlist not only in the army but also in the medical corps. Veterans of the South African War, engineers and aviators also enlisted. Those too young for military service and the elderly were among the volunteers.

"There will hardly be any need for a compulsory mobilization of the Canadian militia for service, or of those who have seen active service, but who are not enrolled in any corps," the *Winnipeg Tribune* said. "Offers are arriving in such numbers that it is almost impossible to acknowledge them. The voluntary offers so far received will number over twelve thousand men, horse and foot."

In Toronto, the crowds of volunteers and reservists were so large they were described as a mass of humanity. The 2nd dragoons, headquartered in St. Catharines, and the 44th Lincoln and Welland regiment, headquartered in Niagara, were the first units mobilized. All Toronto regiments reported they were ready for duty if called.

In Halifax, militia members had been called to duty the day prior to the war declaration.

All throughout the country, notices began appearing in the newspapers listing the names of those who had enlisted or been mobilized.

Economists estimated war would cost Britain $5 billion dollars. The actual figure was double that, a debt that wasn't paid off until 2015. Canada's war debt would total $2 billion.

"Let 'em Fight"

The European powers hoped the U.S., the largest world power without a stake in the conflict, would intervene and negotiate peace. On July 31, the Chicago Tribune reported the International Bureau of Peace made a request for Wilson to offer mediation. The bureau previously had asked Germany to settle its conflicts.

Although the United States had yet to declare officially its neutrality in late July, the government's opinion was clear. "There is not the slightest intimation that the Washington government will offer its good offices to bring about peace between the warring countries of Europe," the *Los Angeles Times* reported.

A formal declaration of neutrality did not seem necessary, the U.S. government reasoned, unless the war expanded or the nation's merchant ships were threatened. Wilson said he hoped a peaceful solution could be found and that he would make no further comment because the U.S. did not interfere with European political affairs. AP called Wilson "strongly disinclined toward mediation in Europe."

There also was concern over potential embarrassment to the nation's commerce should the first-class shipping powers of Europe go to war. This was because the International Mercantile Marine had inquired whether it could fly the Stars and Stripes instead of the Union Jack. A flag switch violated law, and Wilson said he would take the matter to Congress should American commerce be "menaced."

"Neutrality His Policy"

Americans were warned in advance that a formal declaration of neutrality was legally binding and violations were a serious matter. What neutrality meant was published in great detail in U.S. newspapers.

"American citizens while in this country cannot accept commissions from either combatant," the guidelines in the *Los Angeles Times* read in part. "They may not enlist to fight abroad, nor may they equip any vessel of belligerents."

Of course, many Americans did violate the law and enlisted in other nations. In Paris, so many Americans were interested in fighting for France that an American corps was under consideration.

One of the most famous of these volunteers was Eugene Bullard, a Georgian who was half African-American and half Native-American. He joined the French Foreign Legion and later the French Air Force, becoming history's first black fighter pilot. He was awarded numerous medals including the Croix de Guerre, the highest French military honor, and flew 20 missions. When the United States joined the war in 1917, Bullard tried to join the U.S. Army, but it turned him down because of his race.

Other Americans fought for Canada or Britain.

"Administration Changes Its View"

By Aug. 2, the administration was singing a different tune. A *New York Times* correspondent reported Secretary of State William Jennings Bryan had made informal inquiries, asking whether the U.S. as a disinterested country could be of any service. The European powers declined. The correspondent did not know how many nations had been contacted, but said the inquiries were prompted by the Hague Convention of 1907, where it was decided international disputes should be settled first by mediation.

After the great European powers were pulled into the conflict, the Wilson administration changed its priority to aiding Americans who were still overseas. Funds totaling $250,000 were appropriated to take care of the more than 150,000 tourists' needs, and U.S. embassies were instructed to help tourists cash their traveler's checks or receive credit.

"The present disturbances in Europe," Wilson told Congress, "with the constant interruption of transportation facilities, the increase in living expenses, coupled with the difficulty in obtaining money from this country, have placed a large number of American citizens temporarily or permanently residents of Europe in a serious situation and have made it necessary for the United States to provide relief and transportation to the United States or to places of safety.

"The situation also has thrown on our diplomatic and consular officers an enormous burden in caring for the interests of Americans in the disturbed areas and makes it necessary to provide for greatly increased expenses."

To the American public, Wilson urged calm. In his statement, he said:

"Of course, the European world is in a highly excited state of mind, but the excitement ought not to spread to the United States.

"So far as we are concerned, there is no cause for excitement."

A TALE OF TWO NATIONS: CANADA, U.S. AND WWI

Part 2: 1915

Ypres: Baptism of Fire and Blood

The Canadian Expeditionary Force had been in Europe for six months, first training in Salisbury Plain, England, and then as a reserve force. The men of the CEF were subjected to daily drills, parades and 10-mile route marches. Most of them had never experienced combat.

"Being under fire for the first time exists, as a psychological problem, only in the most shadowy form until the idiosyncrasies of the individual man have been taken into account," a *Vancouver Daily World*'s medical correspondent said.

He interviewed wounded British soldiers and asked about their first experiences in battle. "Under fire these men found a self hitherto unsuspected, that elusive quality which for want of a better title is called manhood," he said.

A Brilliant Victory

British troops had begun their advance, it was reported on April 20, pushing forward three miles, the largest advance since autumn. The British blew a portion of a 500-foot-high hill outside the city of Ypres, Belgium, away, the *New York Times* war correspondent said. After a fierce battle for the hill, the British were in the perfect position to continue the next phase of the battle plan.

A German capture of Ypres would make it much easier to take Calais. German reinforcements had moved into Flanders with more reinforcements still coming. The *Times* correspondent estimated 500,000 German soldiers were on their way.

Sixty failed German attempts were made to capture what the British dubbed Hill 60, southeast of the city. While the Germans shot 17-inch-diameter shells into the 200-yard-long mound, British tunnel engineers placed mines beneath it. The hill was already a pitiful sight, covered with trenches, sandbags and ground coverings.

The First, Second and Third Canadian Artillery Brigades fired a shower of shells onto the German trenches.

"Canadians in London are elated at the news that the first contingent has again struck a decisive blow for the empire," the *Vancouver Daily World* said.

The headline of the *Ottawa Journal* read, "War Office Reports Gallant Charge of Canadians in Which They Retake Lost Guns, Capturing Many German Prisoners Including a Colonel – Our Men Show Fine Courage," and the subhead asserted "CANADIANS WIN BRILLANT VICTORY."

Details of the brilliant victory came from the war office in London, and the first reports sugarcoated what was to come: The line to the left of the Canadians had been left bare, forcing them to fall back in order to keep in line with neighboring troops. The Germans captured four 4.7-inch field guns, but the Canadians later retook them. These guns normally were kept two to three miles behind the advance trenches. In the process of retaking the weapons, Canadian troops also captured several German prisoners, including a colonel.

Major-General Sam Hughes, the minister of the militia, told the media he had no additional information regarding the battle and that it would take as many as three days before casualty lists would be sent to Canada.

Hughes praised the soldiers, saying they did what was expected of them. And as for what was expected to be a high casualty rate, Hughes said, "...we must be prepared for these."

What the Germans Have Let Loose

Within hours the war news turned sinister. The Germans unleased chlorine gas along a three-mile-line, which caused eye pain and labored breathing as far as two miles behind the line, and temporarily breaking the Allied line.

The gas moved over the ground like a yellow curtain, a 16-foot-high curtain that hovered over the ground like a deadly fog. After about 15 minutes, the Germans determined it was safe and rose from their trenches to move across No Man's Land, stealing dead soldiers' weapons as they went. Men who were injured were told to lie down so they could die "better."

The gas was so powerful it "produced an effect of complete asphyxiation among our troops," the French war department said. However, the department also said that the gas attack had no "grave consequences" and that the Allies had successfully counterattacked. British Field Marshall Sir John French, commander of the British forces, later would say the attack was in violation of the Hague Convention.

After the battle, the German response was that the gas was no more deadly than an attack with mortar shells or hand grenades. The Germans also said they were not in violation of the Hague Convention because the convention only forbade the use of asphyxiating projectiles, and the gas was not released from a projectile. If this were true, some in France and Britain began to think, then it was time for their nations to develop gas weapons as well.

A Belgian committee investigated the gas attack. It concluded that the gas clouds were 300-feet high, light yellow at the top and green on the bottom. The clouds were composed of chlorine and, the committee believed, other gases such as sulphurous anhydride.

The committee also concluded that the gas was unleashed using four methods: by lighting fires and allowing the wind to blow the gas, by throwing canisters of gas by hand, by cylinders of compressed gas, or by shells containing compounds that turned into gas when they exploded.

The Price of Victory

While the gassed French soldiers either died, fled or were knocked unconscious, the CEF was to the extreme left of the Allied line. The Canadians fought the Germans, often hand-to-hand and with bayonets, and kept the Allied line intact. The Canadians also were able to advance forward, taking the guns and prisoners mentioned in earlier reports. The soldiers called what happened, "Hell let loose."

Such events were not capable, the Canadian Press said, without heavy casualties.

At first, casualty rates were grossly underestimated, believed to be a bit more than 1,000 non-commissioned men and officers. This was based on the first officer casualties reports – 66 wounded, 21 killed. The actual figure was six times higher.

"My colleagues and I are deeply lament the long list of casualties," Prime Minister Sir Robert Borden said, "and send our profound sympathy to every home which is plunged into sadness and sorrow by the tidings that reach us from hour to hour."

In many communities people anxiously awaited news. Winnipeg's *Manitoba Free Press* was inundated with phone calls from citizens wanting to know which regiments were engaged in the battle and when the casualty lists would arrive. Many others showed up at the newspaper office to inquire in person while crowds waited outside for bulletins.

"The anxiety of the people served bare the great silent heart of the city," the *Free Press* said, "for in the telephone calls alone there was revealed the anguish of heart and suspense of endless waiting that have endured by thousands of Winnipeg families…. The voices of those who telephone had for the most part a plaintive tone suggestive of a deeply troubled wife, or mother, or father."

People asked for news but dreaded the response, the *Free Press* said. Still, knowing was better than the suspense.

"To those whose duty it was to convey information, there was brought home a realization of the silent sacrifices of thousands of Winnipeg families."

The silent sacrifice would be experienced in countless households nationwide.

Casualty lists were sent to the militia office but were not made public until next of kin were notified via telegraph. Initially, all the media could report was nearly every battalion took part in the battle, but it didn't take long before the casualty lists began appearing in the newspapers.

Men were listed under one of the following designations: killed in action, died of wounds, dangerously wounded, seriously wounded, slightly wounded, not seriously injured.

Some units had been decimated more than others. Of the 1,000 men who comprised the Princess Patricians only a few were left. Princess Patricia's Light Infantry was a battalion comprised of Canadian men who had prior military experience. It trained separately from the CEF and saw its first engagement in January.

Other units with high casualty rates included the Second battalion [men from Ottawa], the Fourth Western Ontario battalion [men from cities west of Toronto such as Hamilton and London] and the Sixteenth battalion [men from Vancouver, Victoria and Winnipeg].

One of every three soldiers from Vancouver was on the casualty list, Associated Press reported.

The wounded included an American, Walter Watt, of Long Beach, CA. He was attached to the third field ambulance of the Canadian Army Medical Corps.

Another American wounded was Philip Sampson, a Chicagoan serving with the Royal Montreal Rifles, who woke up under a pile of bodies covered by mud. After smoking one of his last cigarettes, Sampson heard German rifle fire overhead. He dug himself out of the trench and walked to a first aid station where he received medical care for his wounds.

Valiant Work

The Second Battle of Ypres was hailed by the Canadian Press as the "first great event of its kind in Canadian history."

Borden said Canadian soldiers "have proved themselves the equal of any troops in the world, and in doing so had brought distinction and renown to the Dominion."

People throughout the nation expressed his sentiments, and newspapers throughout Canada praised the brave troops and the part they played in history.

"The men of the Maple Leaf set their teeth to dare all by a charge, which was a magnificent feat of arms and will stand the annuals of this war, no matter what it yet may bring," James Louis Garvin, editor of the English newspaper The *Observer*, told the Canadian Press.

What made the success so amazing was the fact that most of the soldiers were novices who months before had been laborers and professional men.

"But it is considered that the mourning in Canada today for husbands, sons or brothers who have given their lives for the empire should have, with as little reserve as military considerations allow, the rare and precious consolation which, in the agony of bereavement, the record of the valor of their dead must bring," the *Vancouver Daily World* said. "And indeed the mourning in Canada will be very widespread, for the battle which raged for so many days in the neighborhood of Ypres was bloody…"

Newspapers in Great Britain called the Canadians valiant and the pride of the empire. They also said the CEF saved the battle by their actions during the gas attack. London's *Pall Mall Gazette* went so far as to suggest that the blood shed by the Canadians during the battle would bring happiness to the entire human race.

"Mown Down Like Sheep by German Artillery Fire"

First-hand accounts of the battle further illustrated the Canadians' bravery. According to one unnamed soldier, the troops were given orders and took their positions without any equipment other than 400 rounds of ammunition per man. Shortly after midnight, the order was given for them to charge the Germans who were about 500 yards away. They were fired on heavily, the soldier said, but pressed forward.

An anonymous war correspondent continued the tale. The men crossed the Yser Canal on a pontoon bridge and waited until daybreak. Ten minutes after they crossed, a shell burst over the bridge.

"Darkness had come but at rapid intervals the night was turned into day by flares and German shells," Sergeant Bennett told the Canadian Associated Press.

When dawn broke, the war correspondent said, the Canadians saw they were below a hill with the crest around 900 yards away. At seven o'clock, the men were warned not to waste ammunition, and the assault began.

The CEF had been told to be quiet during their charge, but instead the men cheered and yelled as they approached the Germans who, concealed in woods, began mowing them down with machine gunfire.

Still, the men of the CEF advanced, inspired in their work, Sergeant-Major J. Grant told the Canadian Associated Press, by the women and children fleeing Ypres in terror.

The men witnessed the effects of the gas attack on the French, Canadian Press said. While being assaulted by gunfire, shrapnel and other dangers, they encountered men blinded, weak and ill from the chlorine fumes. Some of the Canadians were gassed themselves and described it as an unbearable burning and choking feeling.

War correspondent Roland Hill remarked that the Canadian line "looks like a regiment of cowboys from the western plains." The soldiers had covered their noses and mouths with handkerchiefs to minimize the chlorine's effects. Hill failed to mention the handkerchiefs were doused in urine, which neutralized the gas's caustic nature. In a time before troops were equipped with gas masks, this simple fix helped protect the mucus membranes in the sinuses and lungs.

Reinforcements Needed

While men were dying at Ypres, the *Manitoba Free Press* said "many [are] anxious to become aviators." Looking at the headline 100 years on, the use of the word "anxious" instead of the correct word "eager" is telling. Pilots had the shortest life expectancy of any serviceman during the war.

More than 75 men applied for the army flying service; the majority from Toronto and Ottawa.

To be accepted into the service, men had to be younger than 30 and pass a medical exam. If accepted, they were required to pay $400 for training, $375 of which would be reimbursed once the recruit traveled to Britain.

Men who successfully completed the course received a pilot's certification and were sent to England for additional training.

Canada's most famed flying ace was Billy "Lone Hawk" Bishop. Bishop flew in 1917 and 1918 and is credited with 72 "kills."

The anxious aviators also may have been responding to a report that a German squadron of 15 ships was headed toward Canada to bomb coastal cities. The information, however, came from an unreliable source – a personal letter – and ultimately was untrue.

Canadian infantry reinforcements arrived safely in France in late April after training in Canada over the winter. These men soon would be pressed into service, filling in for compatriots who were wounded or killed.

"Everywhere they were cheered by French and British soldiers, for along the whole Allied line now the story of the Canadian heroic defense has travelled," correspondent Hill said.

Remembering the Dead

By April 27, the troops were relieved and sent behind the line where they were expected to be given up to two weeks of rest. A report the next day, however, contradicted this. It stated the Canadians were still fiercely fighting along a five-mile stretch from Pilikem to the Furness-Ypres canal.

A memorial service was scheduled for April 29 on Parliament Hill in Ottawa. The outdoor service would be nondenominational and mirror a service held at Valcartier, the Quebec military training camp, before the first contingent left. Religious leaders, politicians, public dignitaries and soldiers in training were expected to attend.

On the day of the service, 20,000 people showed up, and the entire hill was occupied. Rev. W. T. Herridge, moderator of the general assembly of the Presbyterian Church of Canada, the nation's largest Christian denomination, presided over the service. In his sermon, he spoke of the dead soldiers' heroism and how they strengthened the bonds of the empire. Prayers and hymns followed.

The service concluded with *God Save the King*, and soldiers in training marched by and saluted. The audience cheered a unit of Canadian Army Nursing Service members.

Another memorial service was held a few days later in London, England, and Vancouver held three in May.

Meanwhile, in Belgium, 16,000 unburied corpses lined the Ypres battlefield all the way to the North Sea. Neither side would grant a truce so that the bodies could be buried, but there was widespread fear the decaying corpses would cause a cholera epidemic. For 150 square miles, not one building was left undamaged.

As the nation mourned, flags throughout Canada were flown at half-staff.

Former Prime Minister Sir Wilfred Laurier told Canadian Press, "The bravery of the Canadians was a credit to Canada and we are all proud of them."

Not everyone was as diplomatic. A war correspondent said, "We will have to kill tens of thousands more Germans before there can be a peace that will justify all this suffering and sorrow."

Saving Those Who Could Be Saved

The nearly 5,000 Canadians wounded during the battle were moved behind the line for medical care. The most seriously wounded were kept in base hospitals on the Continent while the rest were sent to hospitals in Britain.

Many of the Canadians suffered from the effect of chlorine gas, and on April 28, the war office officially acknowledged that many of the deaths were from asphyxiating gas.

The gas attacked the mucus membranes, and those who were unable to escape were overcome with a cough and bloody sputum. Their faces also turned blue from a lack of oxygen.

Thirty-one French soldiers were brought to an American hospital in Europe. They had been shot while fleeing their trenches after the chlorine attack. Their eyes were swollen shut, and they suffered from inflamed bronchial tubes.

"I am lucky to be alive," an unnamed Canadian soldier told a war correspondent from his hospital bed. "My wounds are going on all right; but I cannot get rid of the irritation in my stomach from the fumes. We little dreamed of the power that was in the sneaking, creeping fog-cloud till it wrapped us in its clutches."

Post mortems conducted by the British Army revealed the Canadians who died after chlorine gas exposure perished due to acute bronchitis.

And, if that wasn't bad enough, the Germans were shelling the advanced dressing stations and any location that flew the red cross of a medical unit. One example was the town of Epernay that was occupied almost exclusively by medical units. The Germans bombed it using both shells and zeppelins. One of the zeppelins crashed after being hit by French artillery.

Here are some of the other medical stories that covered during the Second Battle of Ypres.

1. **Mending Bullet Wounds**

The technology of the First World War presented medical personnel with a new problem – the treatment of bullet wounds. Treatment was, of course, not new, but German soldiers were using dum-dum bullets, and they produced horrific wounds.

Dum-dum bullets were normal ammunition that was altered to remove the tip's casing. When these bullets struck their target, they turned and entered backward, causing a larger than usual wound.

In addition to larger wounds, battlefield conditions meant bacteria infected the wounds immediately, and men arrived at medical units with wounds mixed with mud, pieces of cloth, dirt and even manure.

Tetanus was rare, H. S. Souttar, surgeon-in-chief of a Belgium field hospital, said in his book *A Surgeon in Belgium*, an excerpt of which was published in the *Ottawa Journal*. Other infections, however, were prevalent, and at times wounds had such unbelievable odor that medical personnel could barely tolerate the stench.

Wounds were cleaned with an oxygen solution and lightly wrapped. Patients then were treated with air exposure, encouraging the body to heal.

"The removal of the bullets is not necessary or advisable," Souttar said, "unless the bullet is pressing on some nerve, interfering with a joint, or in some way causing pain or inconvenience."

Leaving the bullet in the body is preferable, Souttar said, because removal may cause infection to flare up. He said a bullet left in the body was no more harmful than surgical steel plates, silver wires and meshes.

"It is a matter in which the public are very largely to blame, for they consider that unless the bullet has been removed the surgeon has not done his job," Souttar said. "Unless he has some specific reason for it, I know that the surgeon who removes a bullet does not know his work."

1. Only the Best Will Do

Some of the first Allied ambulances sent to the front were old cars – many limousines – painted military gray with a red cross on the hood. They varied from the working man's Ford to the luxury Rolls-Royce. These cars were pressed into service up to 14 hours a day.

A TALE OF TWO NATIONS: CANADA, U.S. AND WWI

In the war's earliest days, any "rattletrap" was accepted, but the work was proving too much for these vehicles, E. C. Vivian said in an article in the magazine *Motor* that was reprinted in the *Ottawa Journal*. The military sought only quality vehicles.

The American Ambulance Hospital in Paris took out an ad in the *New York Times*. The hospital solicited donations to purchase 10 new ambulances for use at the front. During the first three months of the year, the hospital the hospital's ambulances transported 20,148 wounded.

"For $1,500 an ambulance chassis can be bought here, sent to France, equipped as an ambulance and maintained for six months," the ad said.

Donations were to be sent in-care-of J.P. Morgan and Co., Wall Street.

1. Help Wanted

The first contingent of nurses in the Canadian Army Nursing Service landed in Europe in October, along with the CEF. By April, the second contingent was in Ottawa preparing to leave for active service on the front. The second contingent consisted of 96 nursing sisters, 93 Canadians from all parts of the country and three Americans.

The group arrived not long after the nursing service suffered its first casualty: Marcella Richardson who died in March of gastritis. Even though her death was from natural causes, it made national news. Richardson served as a nurse during the Boer War, where she was awarded a medal for her services, and was one of the first to volunteer when the Great War started.

Richardson would not be the last Canadian nurse to die. Others would meet more violent ends, dying as the result of drowning or German bombardments, while some would die of disease.

The Canadian Army Dental Corps sought dental surgeons who were willing to serve at the front. Those interested were asked to write or telegraph the chief dental officer in Ottawa.

Applicants were to include when they graduated and from which school, their age, general experience and whether they were married or single.

Lusitania: Hubris Unsinkable

Nothing would stop some from traveling, not even an ominous notice that appeared in newspapers on April 22. It was issued by the Imperial German Embassy in Washington, D.C., and read:

Notice!

Travellers intending to embark on the Atlantic voyage are reminded that a state of war exists between Germany and her allies and Great Britain and her allies; that the zone of war includes the waters adjacent to the British Isles; that, in accordance with formal notice given by the Imperial German Government, vessels flying the flag of Great Britain, or any of her allies, are liable to destruction in those waters and that travellers sailing in the war zone on ships of Great Britain or her allies do so at their own risk.

The *Lusitania* was a Cunard Line vessel. Costing $7 million to build, it was the world's largest ship, and had won the coveted Blue Riband ribbon for having the fastest Atlantic crossing.

On May 1, the day the spacious ship was scheduled to disembark for Liverpool from New York, first- and second-class passengers were met at the dock by aggressive strangers speaking English with German accents. The strangers warned the passengers not to board.

Several passengers also received telegrams signed by the pseudonyms George Jones and John Smith.

Alfred Gwynne Vanderbilt, the wealthiest man aboard the *Lusitania* with a fortune valued at $70 million, was sent a telegram reading: "Have it on definite authority the *Lusitania* is to be torpedoed. You had better cancel passage immediately."

It was delivered just as the gangplank was being raised. Laughing, Vanderbilt dismissed the warning. Moments after he read the message, the clouds parted and the sun shown on the ship. Vanderbilt took this as a good omen and threw the telegram away.

It had been Vanderbilt's second warning of the day. That morning, his mother Alice called his New York City home, letting Alfred's wife Margaret know of the newspaper warning. When Margaret pointed it out to her husband, however, he found it funny.

"Well, how ridiculous this thing is," Vanderbilt told fellow first-class passenger George Kessler. "The Germans would not dare to make any attempt to sink this ship."

The warnings went unheeded, and the *Lusitania* had bookings for 350 first-class passengers, 600 second-class voyagers and 360 in steerage, numbers that would be revised days later. No one cancelled, although many were nervous.

At the last moment, the ship took on 200 more passengers from the Anchor Line ship *Cameronia*, bound for Glasgow. It was unclear why Anchor was unloading *Cameronia*'s passengers, but it was thought the ship was headed to Halifax or Quebec to transport Canadian troops on the order of the British Admiralty.

The transfer of *Cameronia*'s passengers caused *Lusitania* to leave an hour later than scheduled. Including the crew, 1,918 people were aboard.

Cunard Line general agent Charles Sumner told *The Evening World* that he felt the Germans were simply devising methods to discourage people from traveling Cunard with the goal of putting the line out of business.

"The fact is that the *Lusitania* is the safest boat on the sea," he said. "She is too fast for any submarine. No German vessel of war can get near her. She will reach Liverpool on schedule time and come back here on schedule time just as long as we care to run her in the trans-Atlantic trade."

Someone Did Touch Her

On Friday, May 7, the *Lusitania* was in the Celtic Sea with Ireland's Old Head of Kinsdale in sight. While passengers enjoyed lunch, white streaks were spotted moving across the water. Then something hit *Lusitania*'s side near the second funnel, piercing the engine room. It was reportedly two German torpedoes from a U-39 submarine. Some witnesses said there were possibly three torpedoes, and one crewman believed there had been two submarines.

Captain William Turner ordered the ship to head toward Ireland at full speed, but the electricity soon cut out, extinguishing the lights, engines and elevators.

People below decks breathed in fumes from the torpedoes and began coughing. Some fainted. Those who could climbed the stairs to the deck. The ship was sinking approximately a foot a second, and those who came to the surface on the starboard side found the water already dangerously high.

Lusitania had enough lifeboats to hold 2,640 people. Survivors reported only five of the 35 lifeboats launched successfully. The ship listed to the starboard side, meaning the port side lifeboats were too high to reach the water safely. But even if the ship hadn't listed, it would take an hour to evacuate everyone on board, a marine expert told the *New York Times*.

The ship had been travelling between 15 and 18 knots. Some of the lifeboats were lowered before the engines stopped, and the speed damaged davits and caused boats to capsize. Only two boats launched from the port side. As one of them was lowered, it swung on its davit and fell to the water. The 50 or so occupants were killed.

Survivors said there was no panic after the torpedoes hit. Many believed the watertight compartments would save the vessel, or at the very least prevent it from sinking quickly, so there was no rush for the lifeboats. In fact, the crew said there was no danger and not to be alarmed.

Many of the dead weren't even wearing lifebelts. Some people felt it wasn't necessary while others disliked the idea of wearing them. Those who did put on their lifebelts had a greater chance of survival, and it was estimated that lifebelts saved about as many people as lifeboats did.

F. J. Guantlett, who was traveling on the Lusitania for business, ended up in the water and swam for a piece of wreckage that he discovered was a collapsible boat. Collapsible boats were folding vessels kept aboard ships for emergencies. With the aid of another passenger, Guantlett was able to open the boat, and together they rescued 30 others.

Guantlett said *Lusitania* was listing at that point by about 90 degrees, and he witnessed women and children sliding down the deck.

The ship sunk 20 minutes after being struck, and ended up nearly 300 feet underwater. As the ship slipped beneath the waves, people jumped off. Some were able to cling to wreckage, but others were pulled underwater by the ship's suction.

Canadian Mrs. H. L. Gwyer, a newlywed, was sucked into one of the ship's funnels after a wave knocked her out of a lifeboat. Somehow, steam from the funnel shot her back out, and she was rescued.

Lusitania sunk with her propellers in the air and steam coming out of her funnels, according to passenger Julian de Ayala, the consul general for Cuba in Liverpool.

Guantlett wasn't the only lifesaver that day. Fourteen-year-old Kathleen Kaye helped stewards fill a lifeboat. When one of the men collapsed from exhaustion after rowing at full speed to escape the boat being swamp by waves, she took the oars and rowed the boat to safety.

Not everyone who was rescued from the water survived; many later died aboard the lifeboats.

A Greek steamer and every available vessel from Queenstown and Cork, Ireland, arrived to assist. It took two hours to rescue survivors.

There was speculation after the sinking as to why the ship wasn't beached off Ireland, but the water was too deep and the ship would have had to travel 12 miles for shallow enough water.

Alexander Carlisle, of the shipbuilder Harland & Wolff, said it was absurd to think there was such a thing as an unsinkable ship. Carlisle said that everyone aboard would have been saved had there been two to three hours available for evacuations. One of the disadvantages of the modern ship, he said, was its size and its inability to escape danger quickly because of its proportions.

The *Lusitania* became the 29th vessel sunk or damaged by Germans around the British Isles. The majority were attributed to submarines, although some were the result of mines. Seven of the vessels were from neutral countries – one was American, the others Scandinavian, and all were merchant ships.

The German war zone went into effect Feb. 18 and encompassed all of Great Britain, Ireland and the English Channel. The Germans said their intention was to destroy all enemy merchant ships. The *Lusitania* was indeed in this zone when she sank.

The *Lusitania* carried with her more than 1,000 tons of cargo insured for $7.5 million. A total of $10.7 million was lost including cargo, the ship and all furnishings along with 250 bags of mail.

Watching and Waiting

Cunard's Liverpool office sent several bulletins, but most did not contain definite details.

Friday at 1 p.m., the Cunard Line office in New York received notice of the sinking. The notice said: "We regret to advise that an unconfirmed report is that the *Lusitania* was torpedoed by a submarine at 2 p.m. [Greenwich Mean Time] Friday ten miles south of Kinsale and sank at 2:30 p.m. We have no news yet as to the safety of the passengers and crew."

British newspapers and wireless messages, however, quickly verified the sinking.

Friends and relatives mobbed the New York office, seeking information, while hundreds more telephoned or sent telegrams. Many of those waiting left after being told all aboard had been saved by small rafts.

At 5:30 p.m., the office learned lives were lost and that every effort was being made to rescue the survivors.

At 9 p.m., Cunard's Liverpool office said between 500 and 600 survivors had arrived in Queenstown and nine had arrived in Kinsale. Many survivors needed hospitalized, the message said, and some died en route.

About 100 dead also were transported to Queenstown.

In truth, nearly 1,200 passengers and crew died and 761 survived.

News of the sinking did not deter many to cancel their travel plans. The Anchor Line's *Transylvania* left New York on Saturday with 879 passengers, half of them Canadians, including 23 military nurses. The nurses were told to pray and do their duty. Another ship, the *Philadelphia*, was scheduled to sail the same day with more than 200 passengers.

The German ambassador to the United States, Count Johann von Bernstoff arrived at New York's Ritz-Carlton around 6:30 p.m. Friday and left for the train station the following day. Reporters ambushed him outside the hotel, asking for a comment. His only response: "I'm not here."

Von Bernstoff pounded his walking stick on the floor of his taxicab and told the driver, "Go on! Go on! Damn you!"

Reporters pursued von Bernstoff to Penn Station. Von Bernstoff screamed the entire way for his driver to go faster and was far from happy he was unable to avert the journalists.

The reporters resumed their questioning, asking whether the ambassador thought the sinking was justified. He refused to answer, saying he would make a statement when he was ready.

Although he refused to answer, the questioning flustered von Bernstoff enough he forgot to pay for a telephone call and then went to the wrong train platform.

A reporter followed von Bernstoff onto the correct train and demanded to know why he refused comment.

The ambassador gave a politician's response. He told the reporter the media should question what proof existed a German torpedo sunk the ship.

Von Bernstoff said nothing else, and when his train pulled away, the reporter was forced to exit.

The American Government Reacts

News of the sinking reached President Wilson while he was preparing to golf. His clerk informed him of the news, and a shocked Wilson expressed gratitude there had been no deaths.

Wilson cancelled his golfing and remained at the White House to await further news. It wasn't until after 10 p.m. that he learned there were probably around 1,000 dead.

The president and other senior officials in the administration refused to answer any questions until they learned more facts. Congress members were bolder.

Sen. W. J. Stone, chairman on the Committee on Foreign Affairs, told the press that other than the American dead, the sinking was none of the United States' business. It was a matter between Britain and Germany and the U.S. government had no stake in the sinking of a British ship other than a general interest.

If an American vessel, on the other hand, had been destroyed, the government would consider it a violation of its neutrality rights, he said.

Wilson was, the *New York Times* said, inaccessible. In the hours following the sinking, he had not issued a statement or spoke with Cabinet members. He took his usual Saturday day off, golfing and motoring.

The White House also issued a statement that said Wilson would make no changes to his plans after what had occurred. The *Times* said his behavior conveyed a wish that Americans carry on their lives as before.

Blame Game

New York editorials demonized Germans and called the sinking immoral, cold-blooded murder, a massacre and anarchy.

British newspapers reported that the news was received favorably in Germany. German headlines touted the sinking as a great success while telegrams of congratulations were sent to the German minister of marine.

The Germans felt the sinking was justified because the *Lusitania* carried war cargo, a claim the British government denied.

The German government released a statement after the sinking, blaming Cunard. Germany said it made every effort to warn Cunard, and the ship carried guns and war cargo. *Lusitania*'s owners "knew to what danger the passengers were exposed," the statement said. "They alone bear all the responsibility for what has happened."

Captain Turner told the *New York Times*, he felt *Lusitania* had been unprotected because the British Admiralty didn't send a ship to meet her. An unnamed crewmember confirmed the captain's statement and added that the ship received a wireless message stating mines had been placed 40 miles south of Kinsale and caution was advised. Turner took every precaution, the crewmember said.

Some survivors said Turner was on the bridge and had ordered the lifeboats be lowered. Others said it was every man for himself because no lifeboat order had been given.

The president of the Aero Club of America, Henry Woodhouse, agreed with Turner that a lack of patrol was to blame. He said that reconnaissance from two seaplanes would have been enough to spot the submarine.

The *Lusitania* had spotted the periscope of a German sub in April but escaped before being fired upon, William Marconi, the inventor of wireless telegraphy, said, accusing Cunard of keeping the subject secret.

Marconi also blamed Turner who relied too much on the speed of the ship to keep it away from harm.

The consensus among survivors was to blame the crew. They said ship employees knew submarines were in the area and, therefore, should have taken a different course.

The Living and the Dead

Alfred Vanderbilt, who had a habit of staying in his stateroom for the duration of ocean voyages, was presumed dead. Margaret Vanderbilt waited at home with their young children, advised that there was still hope he would be found alive. The family's representative in London dashed those hopes. Vanderbilt was not among the survivors who arrived in Queenstown. Nevertheless, the family hired a fleet of boats to search for him, but the search was for naught, and Vanderbilt's body was never recovered.

Vanderbilt's situation made headlines, but there were many victims of the sinking described only in generalities in the newspaper reports.

Among the dead brought to Queenstown were mothers still holding their deceased children. Other mothers were rescued, only to discover they were clenching a dead baby. One unnamed mother lost two children and was forced to put their bodies back into the water in order to make room in the lifeboat. As she did, she prayed and wept, and other passengers wept with her. Not long before making it to Ireland, her third child died. They were six and four years old and six months old.

"A heap – literally a heap – of babies were lying on the floor," survivor Oliver Bernard said. "They were almost naked, and their poor little bodies were bruised and cut. Some of them were purple, while some were almost black, and others were yellow."

The *Sunday Herald* of Cork confirmed the grisly sight. Among the dead were 50 infants younger than a year old and 100 toddlers. They had either drowned or died of exposure.

The temporary morgue in Queenstown contained 147 unidentified bodies. The majority of the dead, it was estimated, would never be recovered.

Around 100 confirmed dead were Americans. The U.S. government made it clear it would not pay for the bodies to be returned home; relatives would bear the expense.

Queenstown held a mass burial on May 9 that was open to the public. There were so many coffins the people of Queenstown and Cork could not handle them, and, in lieu of pallbearers, the coffins were transported to the cemetery via truck.

The majority of the survivors were first- and second-class passengers. Survivors were met with great hospitality in Queenstown: hotels and private citizens offered room and board, retailers gave away clothing, and doctors and nurses from as far away as Dublin arrived to assist at the hospital.

The news of the sinking was too much for some, even those who did not witness it. In Baltimore, Marie Ourdan struggled with chronic depression and the previous year suffered a nervous breakdown. She traveled to Europe and returned in December, feeling much better. On the return trip, Ourdan traveled on the *Lusitania*, and hearing of the sinking caused her to relapse into depression. She told her husband she was going to the park to try and get rid of her "despondent feeling." There, she commits suicide via revolver.

What Happened?

The British Board of Trade opened an official inquiry in hopes of discovering how a submarine found the *Lusitania* and why so many died. The official opinion was that there were several submarines that cornered *Lusitania* before firing. The inquiry would prove or disprove this.

There also were other important questions that needed answered:

- Why did the *Lusitania* pass through a war zone without a convoy?
- Was a submarine spotted earlier that day?
- Why was the *Lusitania* traveling at only 18 knots, the speed of a submarine, when it was capable of traveling at up to 26.7 knots?
- Why did the ship keep its usual route after being warned it could be torpedoed?

- Was it true the wireless operators received warning of submarines in the area? If so, why was no action taken?
- How many submarines were there?
- Was there an opportunity to turn toward shore?
- After the torpedoing, why were crewmembers telling passengers to stay onboard instead of heading to the lifeboats?
- Why did the ropes break once the lifeboats were filled?
- Why were passengers not told before disembarking that the ship carried shells and war contraband?
- Why did Cunard not take the warning seriously?

Fifty survivors, a third of whom were American, offered to testify in front of the Court of Inquiry. Written testimony from those who could not appear in person would be read.

These survivors were expected to testify concerning the ship's lack of armaments and how the lifeboats and lifebelts were used.

Members of the American embassy were scheduled to attend and report their findings to the U.S. government.

War Temperature Rises

The Wilson Administration urged the American public not to cause controversy, to let the government learn all the facts.

Secretary of State William Jennings Bryan instructed the American ambassador to Germany, James Gerard, to ask the German government for an official report on *Lusitania*'s destruction. Wilson would act once the information was received.

It was expected the report would admit fault for the sinking. This admittance would leave only one viable option an unnamed official told the *Los Angeles Times*: "The severance of diplomatic relations with that country as a protest against the savagery of its conduct. Such action would be recognized in Germany as the beginning of a state of war."

Illinois Sen. James Hamilton Lewis also urged the American people to wait for the truth so that everyone would be cool-headed when it came time to make a decision. Patient investigation was an American attitude, he said.

Experts speculated that Wilson had two options – he could either declare war or demand reparations for the American dead.

Wilson's Democratic Party was divided between those who felt the public wanted stern action and those who feared action only would succeed in placing more American lives in danger.

Avenge an Act of Savagery

The ship's sinking prompted many to conclude that war was coming to the U.S., perhaps within a year, and that declaring war on Germany would be justified.

"The sinking of the *Lusitania* marks a new stage in barbarous warfare," international law attorney Charles Burlingham told the *Chicago Tribune*. "Until the present war the destruction of a merchant vessel of the enemy without visit and search and without removing the crew or giving them an opportunity to leave the vessel is absolutely unheard of."

"The colossal war has degenerated into one of savagery, disgracing civilization and having no parallel in modern times," was the opinion of the *New Orleans Daily States*.

A man named Charles Stewart Davison wrote to the State Department, telling officials the sinking was "the most recent of a long series of act of war using the territory of this neutral nation as a base of war which have been committed by Germany. The permitting thereof by us in an unneutral act."

The sinking sparked outrage north of the border as well.

"Can President Wilson forever stand aside while international law and international moral standards are cast to the winds by brutal and infuriated people?" Sir John Willison, the Canadian correspondent for the *London Times* said. "If the American republic continues to hold aloof, what standing will it have at the close of the war? If it persistently ignores continuous breeches of international agreements and conventions, what weight will it hereafter possess in the councils of the nations?"

The Only Course of Action

In Times Square, more than 1,000 New Yorkers gathered over the course of two days to wait for bulletins outside The Times Building. The crowd was far from passive, actively debating the war on a platform located on the north side of the building.

Until the sinking, the debaters – who had been gathering daily in the square since the war began – were mostly Germans and Austrians counterbalanced by Irish-Americans. Now, the crowd was predominately anti-German.

Pro-German speakers argued the sinking was justified. The warning placed in newspapers relieved Germany of any responsibility, they said.

Hecklers called, "If you go on like that, you may find yourself in a detention camp before long."

Anti-German debaters said the only logical course of action was war, and this view caused many fistfights with the pro-German speakers.

Two extra policemen were stationed at the square, but they didn't have as much work to do as expected. The crowds in the square were so dense, it made a real fight impossible and most of the violence was relegated to slapping.

Women also joined the debate and spoke "quite freely," although some "fled before the uncensored language of a few of the debaters," the *Times* said.

Letters to the *Times* editors also supported war. One reader, Lyman Abbott, said he remembered quite well how the nation was heading toward civil war during the waning days of the James Buchanan Administration.

"When Sumter was fired on, Lincoln acted," Abbott said. "He did not wait to deliberate beforehand."

Actions Speak Louder Than Words

Former President Theodore Roosevelt said in an editorial that although the sinking of the *Lusitania* had been called piracy, it was different from real piracy; too many lives had been lost.

Germany must be held strictly accountable for its actions, Roosevelt argued, and that meant the United States could not delay to react.

"I said that not only our duty to humanity at large, but our duty to preserve our own national self-respect demanded instant action on our part and forbade all delay," Roosevelt said.

The National Security League, an organization pledged to preparing the nation's military for war, meanwhile, wrote an open letter asking the public for its support.

National defense must be improved, the league said, because the military was inadequate. There were barely 20,000 mobile troops in the U.S. They were scattered throughout the country and couldn't easily be mobilized. In addition, the military was short on ammunition, equipment and officers.

The league called for legislation that would:

- address wasteful military appropriations
- adopt a military policy
- create a stronger navy
- create a mobile army
- better equip the National Guard
- create a reserve for every branch of the military

Membership for the American Legion, meanwhile, more than doubled to nearly 50,000 in the week after the *Lusitania* sank with thousands of applications waiting to be reviewed. The majority of the new members were men with military experience.

"The Legion has reached the point where it would make a formidable corps in service of any army, a corps of trained, efficient and seasoned men whose patriotism and valor is unquestioned," the Legion's headquarters told the *New York Times*.

The Navy League of the United States, whose members included Roosevelt and industrialist J.P. Morgan, voted to adopt a resolution that urged Wilson to instruct Congress to authorize $500 million to improve the nation's naval defense. The funds easily would make the U.S. the world's second largest naval power after Great Britain, buying a fleet of 25 dreadnaughts and battle cruisers.

The organization also planned a public relations campaign with the aim of educating the public on the danger of foreign aggressors. The campaign also would try to elicit new members.

The War Department and the Department of the Navy were secretly preparing for war. A government official told the *Chicago Tribune* that the U.S. was in communication with companies that could supply an army of 500,000 in four weeks. Automobile manufacturers would build military vehicles while clothing and shoe companies would outfit the troops. American ammunition manufacturers and medical supply companies also would be pressed into service. The troops could be mobilized after they were supplied.

The official also said the navy could be prepared within a month, and submarines could be built in three months' time. The only hitch would be finding enough qualified sailors.

If war was declared, the American government would requisition any German vessels in U.S. ports.

"It is no doubt an organized spy system in this country is trying to find out our weak points and it is unwise and unpatriotic to condemn ourselves as weaker than we are," Illinois Sen. James Hamilton Lewis said, "We have a patriotic people in our native born and naturalized Americans. If they are called to the standard the citizen-soldiers of America, under the guidance of schooled officers, will bring forth the victory with honor and glory."

Presidential Opinions

Finally, in a speech in Philadelphia on May 10, Wilson appeared to have made a decision.

"... the example of America must be the example, not merely of peace because it will not fight, but of peace because peace is the healing and elevating influence of the world," Wilson said. "... There is such a thing as a nation being so right that it does not need to convince others by force that it is right."

Roosevelt publically disagreed with this position, saying the time for deliberation had passed and that the nation should stop all commerce with Germany.

"The 150 babies drowned on the *Lusitania*; the hundreds of women drowned with them, scores of these women and children being Americans, and the American ship, *the Gulflight*, which was torpedoed, offer an eloquent commentary on the actual working of the theory that force is not necessary to assert and that policy of blood and iron can with efficacy be met by a policy of milk and water," Roosevelt said.

Former President William Taft, however, thought Wilson was taking the right approach. Taft reminded that it is ordinary citizens who pay when war is declared, both financially and with their lives or their loved ones' lives.

"There are things worse than war, but delay, due to calm deliberation, cannot change the situation or minimize the effect of what we finally conclude to do," Taft said in a Union League speech.

"A demand for war that cannot survive the passion of the first days of public indignation and will not endure the test of delay and deliberation by all the people is not one that should be yielded to," he said.

On May 11, newspapers nationwide reported Wilson would send an official communication to Germany. The communication would ask for an explanation to the sinking of vessels around the British Isles, voice American concern about the events and demand Germany play by the rules of maritime warfare. There would be no request for reparations other than the assumption Germany would make them, and there would be no threat as to what would happen if Germany continued its current behavior.

Problem was the administration hadn't decided what to do if Germany refused. Severing diplomatic relations was an option, but some cabinet members believed that would lead directly to war.

Taft sent Wilson a letter of suggestions, and Wilson thanked him kindly.

But, perhaps, action would not be required. Many diplomates and international law attorneys felt Germany would comply with the communication.

Government officials were so confident the communication correctly reflected public opinion it would "make Roosevelt look like 30 cents."

The official communication, published in newspapers, read in part:

"The government of the United States, therefore, desires to call the attention of the Imperial German government with the upmost earnestness to the fact that the objection to their present method of attack against the trade of their enemies lies in the practical impossibility of employing submarines in the destruction of commerce without disregarding these rules of fairness, reason, justice and humanity, which all modern opinion regards as imperative. It is practically impossible for them to make a prize of her [a merchant ship], and, if they cannot put a prize crew on board of her, they cannot sink her without leaving her crew on board of her, they cannot sink her without leaving her crew and all on board of her to the mercy of the sea in her small boats....

"... The government and people of the United States look to the Imperial German government for just and prompt enlightened action in this vital manner with the greater confidence because the United States and Germany are bound together not only by special ties of friendship, but also by the explicit stipulations of the Treaty of 1828 between the United States and the kingdom of Prussia...."

When Will It End?

For months that spring, newspaper reports speculated on the date of the war's end.

In Washington, D.C., the opinion was the war would last at least until winter. The rationale? The nations at war would be against fighting during another winter. Money, however, would be the biggest factor.

"By the time the war has lasted a year the countries involved, it is conservatively estimated will be $60 trillion poorer," the *Chicago Tribune* said. "Taxation to pay interest on this huge indebtedness will be enormously increased."

In an editorial in the *New York Times* by George Wrong, a history professor with the University of Toronto argued the war would continue because the Allies were far from reaching their four goals and refused to negotiate with Germany.

The four goals were the restoration of an independent Belgium, the security of Europe's smaller nations, the destruction of Prussian militarism, and the return of Alsace-Lorraine to France.

Germany, of course, had its own goals, and it would fight for what it wanted at peace treaty negotiations.

"The gambler who brought on the war staked everything on its issue and, if he loses, he loses his leadership in Europe and his dominions over the seas," Wrong said.

There can be no compromise, Wrong said, only one ideology or the other can prevail. Therefore, the Allies must do whatever possible to strangle Germany until it does what the Allies want.

Part 3: 1916

He's Our Man

Nineteen-sixteen was a presidential election year, and in June reporters across the United States prepared to converge on Chicago and St. Louis for the political conventions.

Chicago, as it turned out, would be hosting two conventions. The Republicans and the Progressives – a faction of the party founded by former President Teddy Roosevelt – had made a very public split. So large was the rift that the headline of the *Chicago Tribune* on June 7, the day the Republican convention opened read, "GOP Leaders Bar TR."

Rooseveltians, as TR's followers were called, felt he was the person with the best chance of defeating President Woodrow Wilson in the general election. Party unity would be necessary to defeat Wilson, but could a compromised be reached?

Some Republicans thought so. They suggested the Progressives, also known as the Bull Moosers, could nominate the vice president if the two factions could not agree on the presidential nominee. Progressives found the suggestion ridiculous.

"If we can't come together on a president," Pennsylvania Rep. Anderson Walters told the *Tribune*, "how can we join hands on the vice president? It would be a great situation, wouldn't it, to nominate two tickets and have second place on both filled by the same man? What next will they suggest?"

The National Republican League, a collection of Republican clubs nationwide, met before the convention's opening. The league's mantra was "party before the man, first, last and always," a mantra that was sorely tested during their meeting as TR's followers chanted, "We want Teddy."

Republicans felt TR's supporters were nothing more than a distraction and that a united party was the only way to save the country from the trials and tribulations ahead. The party needed to regain its prestige abroad and bring back McKinley Administration tariffs, Ohio Gov. Frank Willis said at the meeting.

Tensions were so high between the pro- and anti-TR groups, a fight broke out in the lobby of the Congress Plaza Hotel. TR supporters and presidential candidate and Illinois Sen. Lawrence Sherman's supporters destroyed banners, punched each other, and ripped clothing.

"Vast Coliseum Like a Tomb"

As the Republican convention opened at the Chicago Coliseum, the city was assaulted for days by a torrential rain that turned the streets into streams. A crowd of 16,000 gathered inside, 1,000 of whom were delegates, and their mood seemed to match the weather. They were sullen and uneasy, and the *Tribune* said the atmosphere of the Coliseum was like a tomb.

Outside, scalpers who had been selling tickets earlier in the week for $100 lowered their price to $35.

The keynote speaker was Ohio Sen. Warren Harding who was a nervous and fidgety orator. The *Tribune* meticulously recorded his actions, reporting he made 45 hand gestures, took off and put back on his pince-nez eyeglasses seven times, rose up on his heels 11 times, and wiped his brow once every three minutes.

Harding's reaffirmed the party's platform, called "America First":

- The United States Navy needs to be large enough to protect both coasts from attack.
- An army of substantial size needs to be formed, and universal military training must be considered.
- American citizens in all nations need protection.
- Strict neutrality must be kept.
- All industries must be protected from foreign competition.
- Condemn Democrats for their foreign policy, wasteful appropriations and violations of civil-service laws.
- The influx of immigrants must be controlled.
- The nation must return to a protective tariff policy.

Harding also told the crowd to forget the 1912 split in the party. The Republicans were dedicated to the "progress and glory of the republic" and should focus on Wilson's failings. Any prosperity seen in the nation was temporary.

"The Republican conception [of Americanism, an ideology aimed at creating an American identity] gives the first thought to a free people and a fearless people, and bespeaks conditions at home for the highest human attainment," Harding said. "We believe in American markets for American products, American wages for American workmen, American opportunity for American genius and industry, and American defense for American soil. American citizenship is the reflex of the American conditions, and we believe our policies make for fortunate people for whom morale, material and educational advancement is the open way."

The speech, the *Tribune* said, fell chill on silent delegates.

After two and a half hours, the convention adjourned.

Three Ballots

Before ballot voting began, the Republicans and Progressives met to see if they could nominate a fusion candidate. Republicans asserted they would not nominate TR, and the only way the Progressives would vote for anyone else was if TR stepped out of the race. If he did withdraw, there were some potential compromise candidates. The meeting ended with no progress made, but the group said it was willing to negotiate again.

Somewhere between eight and 12 candidates would be officially nominated once Harding, the convention chairman, approved the speeches. The men included numerous senators and automaker Henry Ford.

Eight hours of speeches proceeded the first two ballots. Although TR would not become the Republican nominee, he did receive a nomination from New Mexico Sen. Albert Fall and was cheered for half an hour. Associate Supreme Court Justice Charles Evans Hughes' nomination was cheered for 20 minutes, while Sherman's and TR's former vice president Charles Fairbanks' nominations also received an enthusiastic response.

The first round of voting had a clear winner, Hughes, and he was predicted to receive 375 votes during the second round.

Candidates Sherman, Fairbanks and former Massachusetts Sen. John Weeks were the only ones who had a chance of defeating Hughes while also gaining TR's approval. Campaign officials met until the wee hours of the morning, convinced that if they combined forces they could defeat Hughes.

The alliance lasted mere hours. Sherman withdrew from the race, pledging his votes to Hughes.

At his home in Washington, D.C., Hughes refused to speak to reporters, but several people waited in Hughes's office for the voting results.

Finally, on June 10, after the third round, Hughes won the nomination. Fairbanks was nominated vice president. Hughes accepted via telegram, then immediately resigned from the Supreme Court. He planned to meet with the National Committee the following week and then decide on a campaign manager and whether he would go on the campaign trail.

Progressives Fight for Their Man of the Hour

Roosevelt stated his views in an editorial in *Metropolitan Magazine* that was republished in the *Tribune* before the convention.

The country was at a turning point in history, Roosevelt said, and must grow into an organized, modern nation. To achieve this goal, he said, the United States must:

- Have a strong federal government
- Promote business
- Create Americanism
- Balance competition between regulated and unregulated industries
- Have military and naval preparedness for defense
- Realize the welfare of the individual is the concern of everyone
- Must fight against hyphenism [hyphenating one's nationality] because everyone is an American. This was especially true for German-Americans, he said.

Chicagoan Raymond Robins gave the keynote speech, claiming the Progressives would join the Republicans if the Republicans nominated someone whom the Progressives could agree with; otherwise, the Progressives will nominate their own candidate.

"We believe the need and opportunity of the time is such that personal differences, partisan bitterness and local prejudice should be surrendered to serve the nation's highest good," Robins said. "In the midst of changing conditions unparalleled in history, we cannot even forecast the problems that will confront America in the next four years. The chief issue today is one of leadership..."

After the Progressive convention adjourned for the day on June 8 around 5,000 Rooseveltians paraded to the Congress Plaza Hotel. They carried banners reading "NOT Roosevelt or ruin, but Roosevelt to avert ruin." and chanted "We want Teddy."

A bystander who disagreed, grabbed one of the banners before escaping. Undeterred, the marchers continued, before Republican candidate and New York Sen. Elihu Root's supporters stopped them. A fight began, and the Root banners were destroyed. Eventually, the Rooseveltians made it to the hotel and half way through the lobby before the police, billy clubs in hand, forcefully removed protestors from the premises. For 30 minutes, the supporters stood outside the locked doors of the hotel chanting "We want Teddy."

The vote to nominate a candidate was delayed, on TR's instruction, until the Republican nomination was made. He was convinced Hughes would lose and that he had a high change of being the GOP nominee.

After Hughes did indeed receive the Republican nomination, Roosevelt was nominated as the Progressive presidential candidate with Louisianan John Parker, president of the New Orleans board of trade and the cotton exchange, named the vice presidential candidate. Roosevelt declined the nomination, saying he did not want to head a third party ticket. He urged delegates to confer with the national committee. If the committee found Hughes' acceptance letter unsatisfactory, then TR might reconsider for the good of the country.

The committee adjourned until June 25 when it would decide whether to endorse Hughes or nominate another presidential candidate.

Roosevelt intended to retire and spend time with his family. At the end of a press conference held in his home, Sagamore Hill in Oyster Bay, New York, TR said, "And now, gentlemen, I'll say goodbye. There's no use of your coming here again or staying in town. I'll have nothing at all to say."

He shook the reporters' hands, telling them, "I hate to see you go, for you add to the scenic features of Oyster Bay."

Suffragists Take a Stand

Multiple women's suffrage groups planned conventions to coincide with that of the GOP. The National Women's Party, organized by the Congressional Union for Women's Suffrage, met at the Blackstone Theater; 1,200 women attended. The nation's five political parties – Democrat, Republican, Progressive, Socialist and Prohibitionist – sent representatives to the meeting to speak to the women. The representatives were heckled and booed.

Suffragist Harriot Blatch led the women in condemnation of the speakers. "As for Mr. Malone," she said of Dudley Malone from the Port of New York, "he tells us to be patient and polite. We have been both. We have never gained anything by being polite."

She then asked Malone to repeat this to Wilson. Malone refused, saying Blatch could deliver her own message. She replied, "All right, you carry this message to Mr. Wilson. If the Republican Party went out and got the vote for the black man, why shouldn't the voting women help out their sisters in the disenfranchised states?"

Malone again refused. He said he was a suffragist, but that Wilson had the right to his own views. "The president who has kept your sons and brothers out of the trenches in Europe is entitled to your consideration and support," he said.

Carrie Chapman Catt, president of the National American Women's Suffrage Association, which was holding its assembly at another Chicago theatre, said that the Republicans could not support a federal women's suffrage amendment. If they did, she said, the Democrats would oppose it at their convention, and suffrage would become a partisan issue. It was safer to simply endorse the principle of universal suffrage without mentioning the means.

The organization prepared a statement that it planned to present to the Republicans. It read, in part, "We women, from every state, gathered at the Princess Theater, come to you in the name of justice, liberty, and equality to ask you to incorporate in your platform a declaration favoring the extension of suffrage in the only remaining class of unfranchised citizens, the women of our nation."

The day the Republican convention opened, a crowd of 5,341 women, as young as six-years-old to as old as 80, paraded a mile and half in a cold deluge and stiff wind. Despite this impressive number, it was much smaller than the 30,000 who had pledged to make the march from Grant Park to the GOP committee. They carried American flags as well as banners with various slogans:

- Why can't I ask for myself, John?
- The United States means Us and well as You
- Government should know no sex
- A republic that is half free cannot endure
- We want a suffrage plank in Republican platform

The weather cost the parade committee $60,390. The committee intended to only pay $5,000 of the expense, the cost of advertising, telephones, banners, salaries and rent. The parade marchers would pay for the other expenses. Additional expenses included $30,000 for transportation to Chicago, $13,000 for ruined clothing and $10,000 for hotel fees.

The Republican Committee on Resolutions met with the National American Women's Suffrage Association, the National Women's Party and the National Anti-Suffrage Association to hear their concerns. The first group wanted suffrage on the Republican plank, the second group wanted a constitutional amendment giving women suffrage, and the third group was opposed to both, saying the majority of women don't really want suffrage and that the Republicans should not take on a controversial issue.

The subcommittee voted against adding women's suffrage to the plank, but the full committee later overturned that vote. Somehow the committee could not make up its mind. It considered adding a clause stating it was up to each state to adopt women's suffrage. Finally, the convention did add the plank before reconsidering yet again.

In a vote of 35 yeas and 11 nays, the plank was adopted. It read: "The Republican party, reaffirming its faith in government of the people, by the people, for the people, as a measure of justice to one-half of the adult people of the country favors the extension of the suffrage of women, but recognizes the right of each state to settle this question for itself."

Catt said that although the suffragists didn't get everything they wanted, it still was a victory.

At a ball held by the Republican Women's Association of Illinois, female convention delegates gathered. When a male attendee said he disagreed with women's suffrage because a woman wouldn't vote if given the chance, Grace Trout, one of the honored guests, replied that any woman who didn't vote when able would be in good company with the 7 million non-voting men.

Some businesses, like Chicago laundry Davies, decided to take advantage of the suffragists' cause. Its clever ad began:

"Women who advocate for equal rights are frequently told that their place is in the home.

"Some men think that women should be happy with nothing to do but cook, wash dishes, scrub, sweep, dust, and do the family washing.

"We believe many women could do more good for humanity if they could be relieved of these duties."

Davies then sold its services as being better than what a housewife could do.

Many of the suffragists supported TR because he was in favor of women's right to vote. The Hughes nomination caused some confusion, as the justice had not publicly stated his views. The National American Woman Suffrage Association tried, unsuccessfully, to get him to comment.

The cause now turned its attention to the Democratic Convention the following week in St. Louis. There, the association planned to line the route between the Hotel Jefferson – where the Democratic national committee was staying – to the St. Louis Coliseum for a silent protest.

A TALE OF TWO NATIONS: CANADA, U.S. AND WWI

The women wore white, with yellow parasols and yellow sashes that read "Votes for Women." As part of the demonstration, a woman dressed as the goddess of liberty stood on a dais surrounded by 13 women in white representing the 12 states and one territory that allowed women's suffrage. On one side of them, stood women in gray, representing the partial suffrage states, and on the other side, stood women in black and shackles represented the states where women had no voting rights.

The demonstration would successfully get a constitutional amendment in favor of women's suffrage on the Democratic plank. Or so the association thought. The majority of the Resolution Committee members were against the plank. Some members wanted a plank similar to the Republicans' while others were against suffrage altogether.

The final plank read: "We recommend the extension of the franchise to women of the country by the states upon the same terms as to men."

This did cause much ruckus and argument when approved.

Catt was disappointed with the Democrat's view, which she called the president's plank, and declaring the Republican's and Progressive's much better. Other suffrage groups were equally disgusted. Ann Martin, from the Women's Party, said her group would be encouraging the 4 million women in the dozen enfranchised states to vote against Wilson.

Suffrage groups from the South, however, disagreed and felt any inclusion in the plank was progress.

"President Wilson cannot be intimidated by the swish of women's skirts," Texas Gov. James Ferguson said. "He cannot be threatened by a few hundred militant woman scattered over the country who say they will turn 4 million votes against him…. Do we want to entangle our women folk in the meshes of corrupt politics?"

Other men where heckled for supporting suffrage. Nevada Sen. Key Pittman heckled back. "You are the sort who listen to the denunciation of women. And are you men who are willing to listen to denunciation of women, afraid of the truth?"

Catt was not willing to sit silent. She sent a telegram to Wilson, asking his view on suffrage. She also planned a trip to Washington to, along with 50 other women, lobby Congress for the passage of the Susan B. Anthony constitutional amendment.

Short and To the Point

Before the Democratic convention opened, there was controversy. The Democratic National Committee was not happy with Wilson's decision to appoint former New York Gov. Martin Glynn as temporary party chairman and Kentucky Sen. Ollie James as permanent chairman. The committee felt slighted it was not consulted first.

Wilson also would send someone to the convention to act as his personal representative.

The Democratic platform was not expected to be completed until shortly before the June 14 start of the convention. It was expected to focus on the "the unparalleled good times" from the influx of business into the country since the start of the Great War, according to the *Chicago Tribune*. It also was expected to focus on how Wilson had kept the nation out of the war.

The Republican platform, a member of Wilson's cabinet told the *Tribune*, "is the weakest, most colorless document which has been presented in a long time. It is lacking in specific character which is essential to a real platform." The Democrat's platform, by comparison, would be full of color, he said.

The final platform:

- Uncertainty must be removed so businesses can succeed
- Tariffs bring in necessary revenue
- Americanism and protecting the rights of American citizens
- Military preparedness
- Secure peace for the world
- Establishing and maintaining a close relations with other Western Hemisphere republics
- Supporting a stable, responsible Mexican government
- Establishing a merchant marine
- Developing and preserving natural resources
- Investigating and planning ways to make agriculture more profitable
- The construction of good roads and the development of waterways
- Establishing employee protections
- Enactment of the Federal Child Labor Law
- The establishment of federal tuberculosis sanatoriums for the poor

- Self-government for the Philippine islands
- Modernization of the federal penal system

All the delegates arrived late on the opening day, with most arriving about 10 minutes before the convention was called to order, and outside the Coliseum the streets were crowded. Many of the state delegations arrived with marching bands.

For half an hour, delegates paraded up the aisle with banners. Finally, National Chairman W.F. McCombs called the convention to order. In his speech, he praised the Democrats while criticizing the Republican Party for lying to the American people and for also deceiving itself. He also predicted that Wilson would win re-election, a prognostication that received 16 minutes of applause.

Glynn gave the keynote speech, highlighting Wilson's role in keeping the nation neutral amidst world war.

"And today in this hall, so that all the world may hear, we proclaim that this American policy that the present administration pursues with patriotic zeal and religious devotion while Europe's skies blaze red from fires of war. Europe's soil turns red from blood of men. Europe's eyes see red from tears of mourning women and from sobs of starving children."

Several names were brought forth for vice presidential consideration. The concern was not who could bring the ticket the most votes, but who was best suited to become president should Wilson's health fail.

Shortly before midnight on June 15, Wilson was officially re-nominated. New Jersey Attorney General John W. Wescott, who praised Wilson for putting the nation to work and making it more prosperous, placed the nomination before the delegates. He also praised Wilson for keeping the U.S. out of the war.

"Therefore, my fellow countrymen," Wescott said, "not I, but his deeds and achievements; not I, but the spirit and purpose of America; not I, but the prayers of men; not I, but civilization itself nominates to succeed himself to the presidency of the United States, to the presidency of a hundred million free people, bound in impregnable union, the scholar, the statesman, the financier, the emancipator, the pacificator, the moral leader of democracy, Woodrow Wilson."

There was one rabble-rouser, Illinois delegate Robert Burke, who voted against the president because the Wilson administration took Britain's side in the Great War.

Vice President Thomas Marshall was re-nominated moments later with no objections.

After several hours of speeches, a banner portraying Wilson was unfurled followed by patriotic demonstrations. Wilson listened, via telephone, and responded, "I am very grateful to my generous friends."

The platform was adopted the next day, and the convention concluded one day ahead of schedule.

The Bloodiest Day

What is now the Canadian province of Newfoundland and Labrador was an independent dominion in 1916, ruled by its own parliament and prime minister but bound to the British Empire.

When the Battle of the Somme opened on July 1 – the bloodiest day in British military history and one of the bloodiest battles ever to be fought – the Canadian Corps was not present. It would not enter the battle until September. Newfoundland, however, was there, attached to the British Army.

The Newfoundland Regiment numbered 801 men and was positioned near Beaumont-Hamel, France. The regiment's objective was to join other British forces and take German trenches near the town.

When the order was given to advance, the horror must have been difficult to overcome. The regiment already had witnessed men in the first two waves of the British assault perish, mowed down by continuous German machine gun fire. These men must have known they probably were in the final moments of their lives.

The distance between their position and the German trenches was more than 900 feet. It should have been shorter, but the support trenches the regiment could have used for cover were filled with dead and dying men.

The Newfoundland Regiment advanced, bravely following orders. The result? Of 801 men, 386 were wounded and 324 killed.

Only 68 showed up at roll call the following day.

Curiously, newspaper reports for July 2 and July 3, make no mention of the Newfoundlanders. The Vancouver Daily World did finally mention them briefly, on Aug. 2. The Ayre family from St. John's lost four family members on July 1 – Eric, Gerald, Wilfred and Bernard.

The Allies declared the opening day of the Somme as a failure after the first 30 minutes. That day the British Empire suffered 57,000 casualties.

"One hundred years after their sacrifice, our greatest debt to the young men who were sent to their deaths is historical honesty," Anthony Germain, host of CBC News Newfoundland and Labrador, said in 2016 of the Newfoundland Regiment. "What did the men in the regiment really die for? Nothing."

National Determination

In Canada, July 1 was a federal holiday – Dominion Day. The day marked the 49th anniversary of the founding of the country, which in 1867 had only four provinces, Ontario, Quebec, Nova Scotia and New Brunswick. By 1916, all the other provinces had entered into confederation with the dominion, except for Newfoundland.

The day commemorated, the Winnipeg Tribune said, the launching of a constructive policy, a nation formed not by revolution but by a long considered plan. The newspaper acknowledged the fledgling nation had a population of approximately 8 million and that its best days still were ahead.

Prime Minister Robert Borden in his Dominion Day speech praised the troops, saying the long casualty lists brought the nation sorrow, but also proved Canadian soldiers showed endurance and valor.

"As we approach the conclusion of our second year of war, the tidings from all the battlefronts of the vast theatres in which the Allied armies meet the enemy are more encouraging than at any time during the past twelve months," Borden said. "We look forward with every hope to successes even more striking, which will bring still nearer the victory for which we are striving and the ending of this terrible conflict."

A Glorious Victory, But At What Cost?

It may have been censorship or a case of war weariness. Whatever the reason, Canadian newspapers were occupied everywhere but the Somme Offensive. The *Winnipeg Tribune* was holding a beauty contest, the price of food was on the rise in British Columbia with bread spiking to 7 cents a loaf, and prohibition was about to go into effect in Ontario.

When the Canadian Corps entered the conflict at the Battle of Flers-Courcellette in September, the event received considerably less coverage than the Second Battle of Ypres did nearly a year and a half before.

Perhaps it was because the home-front problems were numerous:

S.H. Ramage claimed the nation's widows were forced to support their children with whatever work they could find because once a husband died the Canadian Patriotic Fund and the war department stops paying survivors.

T.S. Baxter, chairman of the Vancouver branch of the fund, countered this claim. He said the fund continued to pay widows and the war department's separation allowance carried on until the widow received her military pension. The federal government guaranteed a pension of $35 a month per widow and $6 a week per child until boys turned 16 years old and girls turned 17.

Labor shortages were many. Incoming Director-General of National Service Sir Thomas Tait proposed the registration of adults and the mobilization of women for industrial service. Hundreds of women already were working in Toronto factories, but Tait said his system would recruit thousands more.

It wasn't just Tait who felt women could do more. J.C. Kemp, a member of the British Columbia Consumers' League and several Vancouver women's organizations, claimed Canadian women made it difficult for the nation to prosper. Women are too fond of imported, foreign goods and thus not supportive of domestic industry and jobs; if they would purchase more domestic goods then the labor shortage would disappear, she said.

"'Made in Canada' is destined to be THE slogan in our country from now to the end of time; for unlike that of 'Made in Germany,' it is written in the blood of our heroes," Kemp said.

A meeting between the Imperial Munitions Board and manufacturers attempted to brainstorm other solutions for the labor shortage that they would present to the federal government. Their suggestions were to close public works under construction, put women to work in munitions and other industries and to temporarily suspend the Alien Labour Act, legislation that prohibited companies from hiring foreign employees and bringing them to Canada.

The Great War Veteran's Association was formed from the Returned Soldiers' Association and the Army and Navy Veterans. The association's task would be to assist soldiers as they were demobilized.

While demobilization was imminent for the severely wounded, so many men were being sent overseas that only 60,000 would remain in Canada over the winter, compared to 100,000 the year before. The men would train in England and be moved to the front in the spring. The towns and cities that would house the military units for the winter would be announced later in the year.

In an effort to recruit more men for military service, a government committee was formed to find men who were younger than 40 and working in government jobs. The men would be persuaded to join the military, and their jobs would be given to an older man or a woman. The committee also would limit the number of exemptions for military service, but said it would not seriously consider raising the age of men subject to service.

The *Vancouver Daily World*, however, was discussing compulsory service. Great Britain, Australia, New Zealand and South Africa already had implemented conscription. Canada needed 140,000 more men to fulfil its 500,000-man pledge to the UK. There were men available, but they haven't volunteered. When would Canada follow the other nations' lead, the paper asked.

Many men previously had been turned away from recruitment offices because they could not pass the vision test, so the eye test was changed, making it easier. Starting in September, men who could read a thick, black letter measuring 1.25 inches from a distance of 20 feet with both eyes and without glasses would be eligible for the infantry. Men who could read the letter from that distance with their right eye and a 3.5-inch letter with their left eye also were eligible. Men who could read a 3.5-inch letter with their right eye and a 1.25-inch letter with their left eye would be eligible for the medical corps, forestry battalions, engineering, the service corps and as drivers.

Dominion Minister of Public Works Robert Rogers warned Canada's biggest issue wasn't having been unprepared for war, it was being unprepared for peace.

"We must get into a position at once, without sacrificing anything we are now doing to bring the war to an early and victorious end, for the commercial war which will be waged no less bitterly when Germany is crushed," he said.

Rogers said the nation must be prepared for a large influx of European immigrants once the war ended who would need housing. Canada also must be prepared so there is not another labor shortage and must carefully select its trading partners. He advocated for the construction of a national, transcontinental highway.

The Biggest Day in Two Months

Sept. 15 was called the biggest day of the Somme Offensive since its opening day. Several villages were in Allied hands, and thousands of German soldiers were taken prisoner.

It was so easy, the war reports said, the Canadians who recently had been transferred from the Ypres salient, could practically walk to their objective. They secured 1,500 yards at the village of Courcellette and captured German guns along with 1,200 prisoners.

War correspondent Roland Hill said, "Take the triangle from Pozieres, which made fame for Australians to one side along the Bapaume road on level with Courcellette, then Courcellete, to four or five hundred yards to the left of Mouquet farm, for a front of both area and triangle, then back to Pozieres through battered German trenches, all of which were gained at [the] price of Canadian blood, and you have the area which is the Dominion's share in this greatest battle of the war.

"It is a human wedge which represents Halifax to Victoria that has done it."

Canadians nicknamed their section of the Somme Offensive "Death Valley."

Associated Press correspondent Frederick Palmer discovered men from all parts of Canada were taking part in the offensive and so were many Americans enlisted with the Canadian forces. The men were collectively nicknamed the Byng Boys after their general, Julian Byng, and after the song "The Byng Boys are Here."

It was raining the day of the attack on Coucellette, and the men were plastered with mud, but triumphant, Palmer said.

Articles painted a picture of the Germans cowering in fear at the prospect of battling the Canadians.

"We got the Germans on the jump in Courcellette," a Toronto soldier told Palmer. "He was not expecting us, and he is much easier to fight when he isn't."

"Our boys did great work with the bayonet," an anonymous officer told a war correspondent. "The Germans scooted like rats and the shell holes were full of them. The capture of the sugar factory on the outskirts of Courcellette was a smart stroke. Our boys crept up just after daybreak, utterly surprising the enemy, all of whom were taken prisoners or fled."

Indeed, 11 Canadians received decorations for their service – two were given the Distinguished Service Order and nine the Military Cross.

Borden praised the Corps' accomplishments in a telegram sent to Byng. "We send you and your officers and men warmest congratulations," Borden said.

Byng, who was British, answered, "I am proud of the Canadians under my command and of the skill and courage with which they have fought. We feel that our success is largely due to the support and encouragement we have received from Canada."

The first casualty reports estimated the Corps had 1,200 wounded, 400 killed and 300 missing.

Casualties were heavy in many areas, with newspapers receiving death notices twice or more per day that filled columns of newsprint.

Casualties from the beginning of the war through Aug. 31, totaled 37,861: 27,212 wounded, 25 percent of whom would return to service, 1,282 missing or taken prisoner, 5,998 killed in action, 2,248 dead from wounds, 723 presumed dead, and 398 dead from illness.

Meanwhile, wartime expenditures also were mounting. The Canadian government was spending $700,000 domestically and $1 million overseas daily. The largest expense, at $12 million monthly, was pay and separation allowances.

Terrific Metal Monsters

Courcellette also saw the debut of a new weapon of war. It was called a weird armored car, a land dreadnaught, an unearthly monster and a walking-automobile-machine-gun-fort.

The new weapon was used to travel across No Man's Land and fire on the Germans, surprising them with great success.

"Of course we surrendered, those of us who were alive," a German prisoner told a British war correspondent. "Our machine guns turned loose on it. But the bullets were only blue sparks on the armor."

The sight of the dinosaurs returning to life could not have been more amazing, a special report to the *Vancouver Daily World* said.

The army had a slang term for the new weapon, a tank, but the report said they more closely resembled worms and armadillos.

"The 'tanks' have added an element of humor which put the [British] army, through all its ranks, into a festive mood," the report said.

Too Close to Call

On Election Day in the United States, Nov. 7, both Democrats and Republicans were confident of victory. Wilson was in Princeton, New Jersey, staying at his home, Shadow Lawn, and Hughes was in New York City, staying at the hotel that served as his campaign headquarters. Hughes would vote prior to breakfast, around 7 a.m., and both candidates would wait with their families to hear the returns.

If states' voter registration records were to be believed, Hughes was going to win in a landslide. Nationally, there were 10.9 million registered Republicans, 8.7 million Democrats and 569,537 Progressives.

Bookmakers on Wall Street were extremely busy. One million dollars had been wagered the day before Election Day alone and about $7 million total. The largest bet came from a man who would lose $300,000 if Wilson lost. The odds were 10 to 9 that Wilson would win and 10 to 7 on Hughes.

The weather was expected to be mild and dry in most parts of the country. This hopefully would drive up voter turnout that had been plummeting for decades. During the 1912 race, voter turnout was expected to be between 17 million and 18 million men. However, turnout was 3.5 million less, and this figure is 11 million less than the total number of males of voting age in the country and represented only 15.7 percent of the population.

Taxes and other financial remedies had been suggested as a means of increasing turnout.

"The compulsory vote advocate of today sees in the decline in the ballot a drifting surely to a government of a few people by a few people for a few people," the *Washington Post* said.

Both Sides Declare Victory

The early returns showed a Hughes lead. Wilson remained cheerful and went to bed confident the western states would swing the vote in his favor.

Hughes napped until early evening. The telegraph machine in the hotel was busy for hours, and Hughes was pleased by what he saw, although he gave no official statement. A large electric sign visible from the hotel also showed returns. When Hughes went to bed for the evening at 1:30 a.m., both he and his family believed he had been elected.

In Washington, 100,000 gathered gleefully in the streets outside the city's newspaper offices to hear results and did not disperse until it looked like a Hughes victory. The crowds mostly were problem-free with less disturbances than in past election years, the exception being pickpockets and a few minor car accidents on Pennsylvania Avenue.

Despite the confidence on both sides, Wednesday morning the election results were too close to call and both parties claimed victory.

"We ask only what is fair," Republican committee chairman William Willcox said. "We only want what we are entitled to, and what we are supposed to have."

Both parties were in constant communication with the states, hoping to hear updated results.

The fact the final votes weren't tallied didn't stop newspapers from calling a winner. Some declared Wilson victorious. The *Washington Post* called the election for Hughes.

Radio towers in Arlington, Virginia, transmitted the message to the world that Hughes had won the election and messages of congratulations were received in return.

Democratic Party leaders refused to concede, reminding the media of the election of 1892 that was too close to call until the next day.

Depending on whose estimates were to be believed, Wilson had as few as 270 electoral votes or as many as 313. Hughes had an estimated 284.

Wilson was winning in Ohio by 9,939 votes, but more than 3,000 precincts had yet to report. Many other states also had yet to finish counting votes.

Both parties waited, and two days after the election, the outcome still was uncertain.

Contested Election

The Democrats instructed Connecticut to begin a recount and would do the same for other close states. The Republicans asked the same in New Hampshire.

Willcox said a recount would be demanded in every state where the election was so close that a mistake could sway the final tally.

The Republicans also were preparing to take the case to court. The Republican National Committee hired former Attorney General George Wickersham to lead the legal team. He sent telegrams to several states' departments of justice warning them the election likely would be contested. No legal steps, however, would be taken until the recounts ended.

Should no candidate win the 266 electoral votes needed to secure the presidency, the U.S. House of Representatives would select the winner, just as it had done in 1876 when it decided the election for Rutherford Haynes over his opponent Samuel Tilden. The Senate would decide the vice president.

If the House failed to decide the matter by March 4, then the Senate's selection for vice president would become president.

Congressional action would not be needed, with California being the deciding factor. Fifty hours after the polls closed the vote count was in, and the state went to Wilson. This gave the president 269 electoral votes, as of Saturday, and he was winning the nation's popular vote as well by 403,312 votes.

On the streets of Washington, relieved Wilson supporters demonstrated happily. The police who guarded the White House also expressed joy that the man who often greeted them by name had won re-election.

The Democrats also won the majority in the House and Senate.

Friday, the Republican National Committee began shuttering its New York City headquarters, and the Hughes campaign headquarters began doing the same on Sunday. Two prominent Republicans refuses to acknowledge the party had been defeated – Willcox and Hughes. Four states still were counting votes, but their electoral tally was small, only 27 collectively. Nonetheless, both men refused to concede until the final vote was counted.

In his first speech after re-election, Wilson said, "I want to say that now the campaign is over, we must think of only one thing, and that is not of parties, but of the interest of the great country we all love. Let us forget all our difference and unite for common service. Only in that way can we work for the great nation that has given us liberty and peace."

A TALE OF TWO NATIONS: CANADA, U.S. AND WWI

Part 4: 1917

The Climate Changes

President Woodrow Wilson had run for re-election in 1916 on the slogan, "He kept us out of the war." However, less than a month after his second inauguration, it was clear he had only *temporarily* kept the U.S. out of the Great War.

Public opinion, too, had started to change. Newspapers were filled with reports of torpedoed and sunken ships and of German espionage networks, even German infiltration of local and state governments. Los Angeles, especially, was seen as a draw for spies. It was the southwest capital of German espionage, the *Los Angeles Times* said, and many deals had been completed between Germany and Mexico.

Mexico, which still was in the midst of revolution, was viewed as a potentially hostile neighbor. Also, in February, the British intercepted a telegram between Germany and the German ambassador to Mexico. The coded telegram instructed the ambassador to offer Mexico the states of Arizona, New Mexico and Texas in exchange for supporting Germany should the U.S. declare war. The decoded message was published in American newspapers in March.

"Southern California is literally alive with foreign agents, enemies to the country," the *Times* said, "who have worked with almost open contempt for the government [secret service] agents who are trying to control and watch them. The truth sounds more like the outpouring of a penny dreadful than everyday fact. But it is needed only to remember that England seethed with just such stories until a day before the German Army went pounding down through Belgium and almost, but not quite, reached its objective, the city of Paris."

War Drums Pounding

Wilson was scheduled to appear before Congress on April 3, and when he did, it was expected he would appeal to the nation to support a war against the German Empire. Declaring war was not a decision that came easily.

"This man in the White House, this man of heavy burdens, did not reach the decision of such a fateful import to the American people without considering every phase of the terrible situation in which the nation has been placed by the ill-judged acts of war of the German government and the agents acting under its instructions," *Times* correspondent John Callan O'Laughlin said.

Wilson tried to bring peace, O'Laughlin said, but Germany started a systematic murder campaign aimed at destroying every neutral country. Only a beaten Germany would make the U.S. safe, as beating Germany would destroy its militaristic ambitions, O'Laughlin said.

Germany was unfazed by the prospect of war with the United States, a special dispatch to the *New York Times* said, and had considered war with the U.S. a foregone conclusion. Germany, the dispatch said, preferred war to stopping its unrestricted submarine warfare.

In addition, Germany already considered itself at war with the U.S. since diplomatic relations had been severed Feb. 3.

Wilson was under the belief that he could have declared war two years prior, when the *Lusitania* was torpedoed, but that Americans had not been psychologically ready. Instead, he waited until the people realized the U.S. had to battle autocracy and that German war methods were inhumane.

Hawks and Doves

The American Committee on War Finance, a pacifist group, proposed that the entire cost of a war should be placed on the shoulders of those making more than $5,000 annually. If this was not done, the group said, the burden of paying for a conflict would be on the nation's working class.

The group's proposal was for an income tax of 2.5 percent on incomes from $5,000 to $10,000. Incomes higher than $10,000 would be taxed on a sliding scale, starting at 10 percent, with no one permitted to have a net income higher than $100,000.

"We do not believe that any real patriot wants the poor people of the nation to bear the burden of the cost of war in addition to the burden of fighting," group leader Amos Pinchot said.

The group also called for limits on how much a company could profit from the war.

Pacifists' views were largely ignored. In Washington, D.C., members of the Emergency Peace Federation came to the capital by the trainload, but they were forbidden to demonstrate or march.

Washington had reason to be cautious. In Baltimore and Philadelphia, pacifist demonstrations had turned violent and were met with opposition.

Pacifists who tried to speak directly to Congress members usually received simply a nod or a noncommittal response. One pacifist, Alexander Bannwart, who approached Massachusetts Sen. Henry Cabot Lodge, however, was met with a fist to the jaw from the senator and a beating from a Senate messenger boy. Bannwart was arrested for starting the fight, an allegation he denied.

"It is well for the country to take notice," Lodge said, "that those who claim to be trying to keep the country out of warfare are among the most intolerant of citizens, and they do not hesitate to attack those who hold different opinions."

The majority of the country eagerly welcomed war.

In Chicago, a public meeting filled the city's auditorium. When the facility filled to capacity and the doors closed, thousands waited outside. The enthusiastic crowd had only one thing on its collective mind – preparedness.

The crowd was whipped into a frenzy by patriotic songs played by a live band followed by the invocation from a Civil War veteran. Speakers, including Gov. Frank Lowden and former Secretary of War Jacob Dickinson, advocated for preparedness, calling pacifism a shameful doctrine.

Before adjourning, the meeting attendees passed six resolutions:

1. To support the severing of diplomatic relations with Germany
2. To support the government's efforts to protect the populous
3. To urge Congress to pass a universal military training and service law
4. To urge Congress to equip the military
5. War should be conducted with all the nation's power
6. That these resolutions should be presented to Wilson and Congress

Back in Washington, National Guard members and the public, who accused the pacifists of sedition and demanded the Emergency Peace Federation's office be closed, invaded the office the multiple times. One National Guard man threw yellow paint on the headquarters' front window, and it was necessary to place a police guard in front of the building. The majority of the pacifists left the city April 3, believing their efforts were useless.

Woefully Unprepared

Despite overwhelming support for war, there was one glaring problem: The nation was woefully unprepared for it, according to Secretary of War Newton Baker, because the military was grossly undersupplied.

American airplanes were slow and lacked the precision needed for warfare. It would be necessary to build new aircraft using British warplane designs.

In addition, the military was undermanned, and recruiting efforts began even before the war declaration. The navy needed about 40,000 more men to be considered full strength. Men older than enlistment age, women and churches were asked to encourage young men to enlist.

The army needed 500,000 men. Plans already were in place for these troops, but censorship prevented the newspapers from elaborating. The War Department was seeking mainly unmarried men ages 18 and 19, but would consider men as old as 23. There were about 5.8 million men that age in the country, and the War Department was convinced there would be more than enough available men even exempting married man and those who would not pass the army fitness test. The War Department also was seeking 20,000 tradesmen and mechanics for quartermaster work.

Oregon Sen. George Chamberlain, chairman of the Senate Military Committee, had a solution. His universal compulsory military training bill would be brought before Congress. The bill proposed the registration and training of all men between the ages of 20 and 23. The estimated 1.5 million to 2 million men could be called whenever the president needed them.

While registration would be a huge project, the federal government expected city and state officials would help. Certain professions were expected to receive an exception, although that had yet to be decided.

To assist with a shortage of medical personnel, Columbia University's College of Physicians and Surgeons decided to graduate its senior class four months early. The 100 students would study all summer in order to graduate in January.

Joseph Hartigan, the commissioner of Weights and Measures, presented a plan to the Council of National Defense meant to address a labor shortage in agriculture once the war began. He proposed using conscientious objectors and men who were rejected by the military for minor medical defects to work the fields.

Men who had moved to the cities for factory jobs already impacted agriculture, Hartigan said. His proposal would stop the farm industry from further harm. The conscripted farmers would wear uniforms, be commanded by officers and receive a government paycheck.

Military training, too, posed a challenge. The public wanted troops sent to Europe immediately, a move that would be suicidal, a military expert told the *Los Angeles Times*. Instead troops needed to be acclimated and commanders would need to establish command in a section of the front.

"There still are a lot of people who think a man becomes a soldier the moment he gets into uniform and puts a gun on his shoulder," the expert said. "This is nonsense, even if the man happens to be an American."

Army officers agreed. "To be of any aid in the world struggle, they say, only a very considerable force of fully trained and highly equipped and organized troops, with adequate independent supply lines, should go to Europe," the *Chicago Times* said.

The nation also needed money to wage a successful campaign. An estimated $3 billion would be needed 10 days after war was declared, according to the U.S. House Ways and Means Committee. Around $100 million would be used for defense of the Panama Canal and the rest would be used for equipment. If necessary, corporate, income and excess profits taxes would be raised.

Brought Before Congress

Some congressmen were against conflict, but they were a shrinking minority, most politicians bowed to their constituents' cries of war.

"Members who a short time ago were distinctly opposed to any hostile measures against Germany are now ready to stand by the president when he recommends war," the *New York Times* said.

Crowds met Wilson on April 3 as he left the White House to travel to the Capitol Building. The assembly was supportive, singing patriotic songs, but the motorcade took a back route, and the thousands of people who lined Pennsylvania Avenue for a glimpse of the president were disappointed.

Wilson also received positive reactions from most of the senators who applauded his appearance at the dais for several minutes. The senators grew serious as Wilson began to speak, interrupting to applaud only when Wilson said the nation would not choose submission and when he said the United States should declare war.

In his speech, Wilson outlined his case for war, citing the death of citizens and the destruction of property from neutral nations as a result of German submarine warfare. He also called for the military to be expanded, and for the U.S. to cooperate with the nations already at war with Germany.

"Neutrality is no longer feasible or desirable," Wilson said, "where the peace of the world is involved and the freedom of its peoples, and the menace to that peace and freedom lies in the existence of autocratic governments, backed by organized force which is controlled wholly by their will, not the will of their people."

The world must be made safe for democracy, he said.

"But the right is more precious than peace," Wilson said near the end of his address, "and we shall fight for the things which we have always carried nearest our hearts… To such a task we can dedicate our lives and our fortunes, everything that we are and everything that we have, with the pride of those who know that the day has come when America is privileged to spend her blood and her might for the principles that gave her birth and happiness and the peace which she has treasured."

The speech moved many of the senators to tears.

WAR!

The Senate was the first to vote on the war resolution.
The debate lasted 13 hours:

A TALE OF TWO NATIONS: CANADA, U.S. AND WWI

"I fear that involving the United States in this European war will be to commit the greatest national blunder of history," Missouri Sen. William Stone said. "I shall vote against committing this mistake, to prevent which I would gladly lay down my life."

Nebraska Sen. George Norris said, "I am most empathically and sincerely opposed to taking any step that will force this country into the useless and senseless war"

"The issue is not peace or war," Virginia Sen. Claude Swanson. "War has already been declared on us. The issue is whether we shall accept war or abject and cowardly submission."

"This war is a war, as I see it, against barbarism," Lodge said, "panoplied [collected] in all the devices for destruction of human life which science, beneficial science, can bring forth... We are fighting against a nation, which in the fashion of centuries ago, drags the inhabitants of conquered lands into slavery; which carries off women and girls for even worst purposes; which in its mad desire to conquer mankind and trample them underfoot has stopped at no wrong, has regarded no treaty."

On April 4, the Senate voted to pass the resolution 86 to 6 with eight senators absent. All eight were in favor of passage.

The war resolution moved to the House where the debate lasted 16.5 hours and around 100 speeches were given. In the end, the resolution passed by a vote of 373 to 50.

Montana Rep. Jeanette Rankin, the first woman elected to the U.S. House of Representatives, was one of the dissenters.

"I want to stand by my country, but I cannot vote for war," she said. "I vote no."

Rankin was sobbing during roll call, but her declaration drew applause from the other "no" voters. She reportedly was so overcome with emotion she did not return to the House the following day and instead was at home, as the *New York Times* put it, "overwrought, harassed by conflicting emotions, beset by doubts."

The day of the vote, too, the Times painted the picture of a delicate woman barely capable of doing her duty. The newspaper said she was "under great mental distress" and described her as being "on the verge of breakdown." It describes her as nervously fidgeting and practically incapable of speech.

Rankin's friend, Mrs. James Laidlaw, who was present in the House gallery, denied the reports. "It is not true that Miss Rankin wept, fainted, or had to be carried from her seat," Laidlaw said. "She was perfectly composed... When she finally voted, she voted with intense sincerity, knowing that she was not doing the popular thing, but refusing to allow herself to be governed by motives of expediency."

Carrie Chapman Catt, chairwoman of the National Woman Suffrage Party, said, "I predicted two weeks ago that no matter which way Miss Rankin voted she would be criticized. If she voted for war, she would offend the pacifists; if she voted against it, she would offend the militarists."

Upon the declaration of war, two German passenger ships and three German freighters in Boston were seized while the Port of New York awaited orders to seize the 30 ships docked there and at Hoboken, New Jersey. By April 7, 91 German vessels had been seized nationwide, and suspected spies had been arrested.

The Wilson Administration wanted to run the war like a dictatorship, the *Chicago Tribune* said. Wilson wanted the power to dispatch the military as he saw fit. He also wanted censorship and espionage bills passed immediately by Congress.

Congress voted quickly to allow Wilson to use the military and the nation's resources to wage war. It also established a $100 million emergency war credit.

Wilson issued a proclamation that applied to all males at least 14-years-old who were living in the U.S. but were citizens of hostile nations. Those individuals "shall be liable to be apprehended, restrained, secured, and removed as enemy aliens."

The proclamation also listed ways enemy aliens must conduct themselves:

1. Cannot possess or operate any weapons, ammunition or dynamite
2. Cannot operate a wireless device or an aircraft
3. All property in violation will be seized
4. Cannot be within a half mile of any military facility
5. Cannot write, print or publish anything against the U.S. government
6. Cannot commit any hostile act against the U.S. government
7. Cannot live in an area Wilson could designate as a prohibited area
8. Cannot aid the enemy

9. Cannot leave the country without permission from the U.S. government
10. Will not be permitted back into the country if currently outside the U.S.
11. If required, all will be registered
12. Any alien suspected of violating the above will be arrested

The day after war was declared on Germany, Austria-Hungary, Turkey and Bulgaria broke off diplomatic relations with the U.S.

War Preparation

The War Department sent the Congressional military committees the outline of a bill that would establish an army of 1 million men within one year and 2 million men within two years. While most of the force would be comprised of National Guardsmen and U.S. Army volunteers, the proposal would raise 500,000 troops through the conscription of men ages 19-25. Conscription would be authorized only if the number of volunteers was inadequate.

To the surprise of many in Congress, Wilson supported the War Department's recommendations while opposing a system of universal military training.

Now that war was declared, it was believed the war's end was a mere month or two away. Germany, quaking in fear, simply would surrender.

"The fact the United States could in time send a million trained men to Europe will have a strong moral effect in ending the war," financier Henry Huntington said. "...it takes time to equip an army and I am of the opinion that it never will be necessary for us to send soldiers to Europe."

The U.S. was putting forth resources unequalled by any nation in history, the *New York Times* said, organized with Yankee skill and business thoroughness. In addition, the *Times* said, the U.S. Navy, though tiny, was "in strength and efficiency among the foremost afloat."

The predictions of the war ending quickly only would be off by 16 months.

The Germans scoffed at the idea of the U.S. making them surrender simply by the fact America had declared war. Germany was aware the U.S. had a small military and would need time to build a substantial force.

German Minister to Mexico, Heinrich von Eckhardt said, "The only co-operation the United States can offer the governments now at war with my country is [a] moral and financial one, and as the Allies have been receiving such aid from the American people since the commencement of the war, America's participating in the conflict does not amount to anything,"

Other Americans Follow Suit

Other Western Hemisphere nations found neutrality was no longer a viable option.

In Havana, German ships were seized, and Cuban President Mario Garcia Menocal sent a letter to the U.S. Congress asking the body for permission to declare war against Germany. The declaration had passed the Cuban Congress easily, but Cuba, which had been occupied by the U.S. military multiple times since the Spanish-American War, was only nominal independent.

"Cuba cannot appear indifferent to such violations which at any moment may be carried out at the cost of the lives and interests of its own citizens," Menocal said in his message to Congress. "Nor can it, without loss of dignity and decorum, show indifference to the noble attitude assumed by the United States to which we are bound by ties of gratitude and by treaties. Cuba cannot remain neutral in this conflict, because a declaration of neutrality would compel it to treat alike all belligerents, denying them with equal vigor access to our ports and imposing other restrictions which are contrary to the sentiment of the Cuban people and which inevitably in the end would result in conflict with our friend and ally."

Both the House and Senate formed committees to consider the matter, but no opposition was expected from Congress.

Panama committed itself officially to assist the U.S. in defense of the canal, which had been completed only four years earlier.

"As the situation creates dangers for our country," Panamanian President Roman Valdez said, "it is the duty of the Panaman [sic] people to co-operate with all the energies and resources they can command for the protection of the canal and to safeguard national territory."

The confirmation of the torpedoing of a Brazilian steamship, rumored to have been attacked without warning, led many to speculate Brazil would be next in severing diplomatic relations with Germany.

Two months earlier, the Brazilian government had officially protested German submarine warfare and had established guidelines for the maintenance of friendly relations.

"American nations must choose between the only two possible attitudes: to side with the perpetrators of crimes or with the defenders of liberty," Brazil's Jornal Do Comercio said.

On the streets of San Paulo, people paraded through the streets, carrying flags, singing and crying cheers of support for the Allies.

Wartime Hysteria

Patriotic zeal gripped the U.S.

Frederick Summer Boyd, an Englishman in New York City, was pelted with salad and mayonnaise at a restaurant for refusing to stand when the orchestra played "The Star Spangled Banner." He was dining with Jessie Ashley, a suffragist and attorney who had been fined the year before for distributing birth-control information, and May Towle, also an attorney. The women, too, were assaulted

Boyd was arrested and charged with disorderly conduct. The magistrate told him that while there was no legal obligation to stand, it wasn't courteous or prudent not to do so under the tense times.

Wilson authorized the seizure of all the nation's radio stations. Some would be used for naval communications while the rest would be closed. The authorization also applied to amateur radios, and, operating off tips, the army searched for privately owned equipment.

The army also searched homes suspected of hiding explosives.

"Carpets were ripped up," the *New York Times* said, "dressers were searched, soldiers carefully removed the backs of pictures, the owners' private correspondence was read down to the last letter, and at one of the places tons of hay stored in the barns was removed from the lofts on the suspicion that explosives might have been hidden there. Before the soldiers left either of the premises [the two houses searched that day in a rural area] every inch that might have served as a hiding place had been examined."

No explosives were found that day, but a radio was destroyed.

Rumors that the army shot and killed a man were untrue, the *Times* said.

A plan developed by the Boy Scout National Council and approved by the Department of Agriculture and the Navy Department mobilized the nation's 250,000 scouts. The boys would either aid in food production or work with the U.S. Coast Guard.

"The necessary elementary instruction that every young American should have in order to be prepared to play his part in national defense can be obtained by work in the Boy Scouts of America," the council said.

In addition to learning survival techniques, the boys would gain military, moral and physical preparation, it said.

News of the U.S. declaring war soon reached the trenches of France. The news was met with mixed emotions from the Canadians. There was joy at the news, but thousands of Americans were serving in the Canadian Corps, and these men would need to be released if they desired to fight under the American flag. Losing so many men would mean the Canadians again needed to beef up their forces.

Canada, as of April, had enlisted 407,342 men in addition to the 11,050 men in the permanent force and the militia. When reservists were included, 449,074 troops had or were currently serving.

Succeed Where Others Could Not

Vimy Ridge was synonymous with failure. The Germans had controlled the heights since nearly the beginning of the war. Both the French and the British had fought in vain in 1915 and 1916 to capture it.

The several mile-long ridge held significant military significance and also was considered the strongest German position in France.

"Upon it hinges the whole strategy of the enemy's retreat in the west," a military expert told the *Winnipeg Tribune*. "With Vimy firmly held he can swing his line farther south slowly back, until each part of it reaches the position where he has a mind to stand, and he can cover the French industrial districts upon which he depends so much for supplies."

On April 9, newspapers reported British forces were advancing from Arras to Lens in France. The battle, which had begun the day before, Easter Sunday, was predicted to be larger than the Battle of the Somme.

"As I went up the road to the battle lines I pass a battalion of our men who are fighting today, standing in a hallow square with bowed heads, while a chaplain conducted Easter services," war correspondent Philip Gibbs said. "It was Easter Sunday, but no trace of God."

Canadian forces, the newspapers speculated, were participating because they already were holding the line in that area, including the lower reaches of the ridge. This suspicion quickly was confirmed. The Canadians easily captured the ridge, which rose 200 feet above the plain.

On the day of the assault, the Allies fired on the ridge. Firing was a daily occurrence and did not raise any alarm among the Germans. The guns then fell silent for half an hour. When they resumed, the ground shook as a cold rain poured on the combatants. The sky was painted red as guns fired and land mines exploded.

Canadian soldiers left their hiding places, craters in the hillside, and advanced per a plan that was months in the making, though what was once an orchard.

Thirty minutes later, the Germans sent up a flare indicating they needed assistance. German reserve troops were mobilized, and spotted by British spy planes moving toward the railroad station, but no counterattack was made. This was attributed to the Canadians' use of 12-inch guns, the size normally used on battleships. All long-range guns within 10 miles fired on a specific point to keep the German Army at bay.

A Texan, who was enlisted with an Ontario regiment, became the first American to carry the U.S. flag in battle. He attached the flag to his rifle's bayonet. The soldier was wounded but was recovering in a hospital.

It took a mere seven hours for Canadian troops to take the ridge.

"Our men were splendid and are proud that they were counted worthy to furnish a striking force in so important an operation as the recapture of Vimy Ridge," the newspaper correspondent, with the Canadian headquarters in France, said.

"The Canadians, who had one of hardest bits of the front to contend with, are now in complete occupation of the famous Vimy Ridge, even its eastern slope having been cleared of the enemy," the *Nanaimo Daily News* said. The troops also "repulsed German counterattacks on the northern end and eastern side of the slope."

The capture meant the Allies had a clear view of the plain below, and the German supply line now was severed.

Days later, the Canadians took a mile of German trenches south of Vimy Ridge where the Germans had taken refuge as well as "The Pimple," the top of the ridge. Within 72 hours of the initial attack, the entire ridge was cleared of German soldiers.

"The Canadians were not to be denied," the Canadian Press said.

The Canadians now held a new line, from the village of Givenchy-en-Gahelle to the village of Petit Vimy.

Amazing Accomplishments

The British attack at Arras was not as violent as predicted and instead resulted in a dent of five miles into the German lines and the capture of several villages, all of which had been reduced to rubble, more than 11,000 prisoners and 100 artillery and machine guns.

"The spoil in war material is large, and it will increase as the remaining unexplored ground is cleared up," the Canadian Press said.

The Canadians destroyed a German artillery dump and took 3,500 prisoners.

"The Boche must have known something unduly fierce was preparing for him in the Canadian sector, seeing that for weeks past he has been tormented nightly with raids and by day has endured a never-ceasing purgatory of artillery fire," the Canadian Associated Press said. "Despite this, he does not seem to have been prepared for such an onslaught as that which crumbled his front line."

"All accounts unite in reporting the readiness of the Germans to surrender as soon as we come to close quarters," war correspondent Percy Robinson said. "They were subjected to a terrible ordeal for days before the attack. Prisoners tell of the terrible effect of the bombardment and the hardships endured. When the attack came, the enemy, undoubtedly surprised, was taken in a number of cases almost in whole units from dugouts practically without a fight."

Casualty Rates "Light"

It was estimated the Canadian Corps would sustain a casualty rate of one-third.

Casualty rates as of April 11 numbered 89 officers and an estimated 1,500 enlisted men dead, wounded or missing. The usual casualty ratio is one to five, but for the officers that rate was 20 to one. This was considered a light casualty rate.

Official casualty lists, however, had yet to be released by the Militia Department. Protocol was to notify families first before releasing the lists to the media, and families were being cabled as quickly as possible.

The low rates were the consequence of battle preparation, the *Winnipeg Tribune* said. A year prior, the British Empire's casualty rates averaged 900 men daily.

Congratulations

Some historians refer to Vimy Ridge as Canada's coming of age, but is this how contemporary Canadians viewed the victory? It marked the first time all four divisions, about 79,000 men –supported by the medical corps, machinists and other noncombatants – fought together. While "coming of age" is not a phrase the newspaper reports used, there was a definite sense that something extraordinary had happened.

Prime Minister Robert Borden told the Canadian Associated Press, "The great victory won is a glorious beginning of the renewed offensive undertaken by the British forces... Canada will be thrilled with pride by this glorious achievement of our expeditionary force."

"The government and people of Ontario heartily congratulate the Canadian forces on their glorious achievement, and thank them for their magnificent service to the empire and civilization," Ontario Premier Sir William Heart said in a message to Gen. Julian Byng. "Our country is thrilled by the great victory which would be an immortal inspiration to noble deeds, and is an assurance of the final overthrow of tyranny."

Praise even came from King George V. "Canada will be proud that taking of the coveted Vimy Ridge has fallen to the lot of her troops," the British monarch said. "I heartily congratulate you and all who have taken part in this splendid achievement."

Some of the greatest accolades came from the soldiers themselves.

A wounded British Columbian soldier said, "The spirit of the Canadians is great. Say, is it not good to be one of the Canadians to take that ridge? ... Shall I be pleased to get home again? Well, yes, when there's nothing more to do in Europe."

With the victory at Vimy, the tide of the war was turning in the Allies favor. Could peace be far away?

A TALE OF TWO NATIONS: CANADA, U.S. AND WWI

Part 5: 1918

Peace at Last

The Great War had been raging for nearly four and a half years. In the final days of the conflict, a period that would later be dubbed the Hundred Days Offensive, Allied momentum pushed Germany to surrender. The other Central Powers – Austria-Hungary, Bulgaria and the Ottoman Empire – already exited the conflict.

During the final 100 days of the war, the Allies won a series of battles and successfully pushed the Germans out of France and Belgium and to the Hindenburg Line. The defensive line had been built over the course of the two previous years and was the final stronghold protecting Germany from Allied invasion.

Armistice with Germany, which had been rumored for weeks, was signed at 5 a.m. Paris time on Nov. 11 with hostilities scheduled to end at 11 a.m. Journalists received word of the signing verbally, and news of the event quickly spread. The exact terms of the armistice would not be released until later in the day but were said to be more stringent compared to those discussed in late October.

Fighting continued until the end. Before dawn, Canadian troops liberated the Belgium town of Mons. The British had fought the Germans at Mons near the beginning of the war, and so, the *Vancouver Daily World* said, Mons was a fitting location for Canada to end the conflict.

The American First and Second Armies were along the French rivers of Moselle and Meuse where they engaged the Germans. "The war was still on," the Associated Press said, "despite rumors of peace."

Germany itself was in a state of chaos. Several major cities, including Berlin, were under revolutionist control, and parts of the empire had declared themselves independent republics. Kaiser Wilhelm II abdicated, and the German Workmen's Council had taken over the government. In the streets of Berlin, crowds sung the "Marseillaise," the French national anthem, and a full-blown revolution soon was expected to begin.

"The arbitrary power of the military caste of Germany which once could secretly and of its own single choice disturb the peace of the world is discredited and destroyed," President Woodrow Wilson said. "The great nations which associated themselves to destroy it have now definitely united in the common purpose to set up such a peace as will satisfy the longing of the whole world for disinterested justice, embodied in settlements which are based upon something much better and more lasting than the selfish competitive interests of powerful states."

The war lasted 1,567 days.

A Joyous Occasion

The news was met with unbridled joy in North America with spontaneous celebrations breaking out in communities small and large.

In Ottawa, the first Canadian city to receive the news, wireless operators feverishly telegraphed other parts of the dominion. The church bells, factory whistles, train whistles and fire alarms that proclaimed the news awakened residents at 3 a.m. Eastern time, and within minutes demonstrations began.

The Retail Merchants' Association gave members and its employees a civic holiday to join in the celebrations or, as the *Ottawa Journal* called it, the work of making noise. Other businesses followed suit and closed as did government offices and schools.

The entire city had simply gone wild, the newspaper said, celebrating with unprecedented enthusiasm. Vehicles were decorated, and people paraded, both on foot and in their cars. As the morning progressed, the crowds and parades grew larger.

"Dignity was thrown to the winds by everyone and many prominent citizens paraded with decorations and horns, and hundreds of women joined the procession," the paper said.

A public meeting of Thanksgiving was held on Parliament Hill at 3 p.m., and all the Methodist churches in the city also planned similar services.

At Connaught Place, the national anthems of the Allied nations were played and people sang. Similar demonstrations took place throughout the city, and crowds burned effigies of the Kaiser.

A TALE OF TWO NATIONS: CANADA, U.S. AND WWI

Three were injured during the celebrations, two from motor vehicle traffic accidents and one from a firework mishap.

In Winnipeg, celebrations started at 2 a.m. Central time, before both the *Tribune*'s special edition and the city's whistles blew and bells rang. Ignoring Spanish Flu precautions, people embraced, and the telephone system reached its limit. Anything that could be used to make noise was put into service – garage can lids, pots and pans, car horns, dinner horns or utensils.

Those going to work found their workplaces closed when they arrived, and an electric sign was install in front of city hall that read "Give Thanks and Rejoice."

Not everyone, however, was pleased with the war's end. "I would very much like to have seen the Allies refuse an armistice and carry the war, with all its devastation, into Germany," a Winnipeg civil servant said. "But the lives of 20,000 Huns is not worth the blood of one Allied soldier."

"It was a wildly hilarious Vancouver which, shortly after the midnight hour, broke into general rejoicing over the announcement of peace," the *Vancouver Daily World* said.

Like Ottawa, Winnipeg and communities throughout Canada, Vancouver celebrated with throngs of people on the streets, noisemakers, fireworks, and song. Even soldiers recuperating at the military annex of General Hospital held a parade, in their pajamas, through the hospital.

American celebrations were just as boisterous and followed the same routine of noisemaking, singing, parading and burning effigies. New York City's celebration went unabated for 24 hours.

The White House was the first to hear the news in the United States. Once President Woodrow Wilson learned what occurred, word was telegraphed to the rest of the country.

The *Chicago Tribune* learned the news via a phone call from the Associated Press. The message was "armistice signed," and then the AP reporter hung up. The *Tribune* was first in the city to blare its sirens, and within 30 minutes the paper's special edition was being sold on the streets.

"Night manager Michael O'Brien had a general telephone alarm sent throughout the house, '*Chicago Tribune* announces armistice signed,'" the paper said. "That was sufficient. The lobby soon looked like New Year's Eve. Every known noise device was soon gathered. Brass cuspidors [spittoons] were grabbed. Flags were torn down and waved."

Overseas, celebrations were more muted. In Paris, it was "quiet joy" as a few bands played and crowds sang the national anthem. Businesses were illuminated outdoors as were streets for the first time since the war began. The populous had a suspicion Germany would pull some sort of trick and peace would not last.

"And yet, despite the bedlam, the incomparable scenes of joy, there were many solemn scenes," the *Vancouver Daily World* said. "Sober garbed women, whose husbands and sons would never return, stood on the curb, a strange mingling of emotions stirring in them. Old men saw the hand of God in the demonstration, and from hospital cots of pain bed-ridden soldiers raised their wracked bodies to listen, and smiles of contentment sank back on their pillows – 'thank God, after all, our sacrifices have not been in vain.'"

Returning Soldiers

Demobilization of Canadian soldiers in Canada, some 35,000 troops, was expected to begin immediately, although no official announcement had been made by the Department of Militia and Defense. The exception would be the men who had volunteered for the Siberian Expeditionary Force, as they still were needed.

Rev. Robert Eadie, pastor of Bethany Presbyterian Church, was concerned for the soldiers who would be returning from Europe. They would need jobs. More importantly, Eadie said, he feared the men would suffer from depression. The nation had promised it would look after these men upon their return and now was the time to fulfil that promise, Eadie said.

Casualties rates printed in the Nov. 11 newspapers totaled 211,358 through Oct. 31 for the Canadians and 69,207 through Nov. 10 for the Americans.

A TALE OF TWO NATIONS: CANADA, U.S. AND WWI

Analysis

The war was barely over when experts and commentators began to analyze it.

Archduke Franz Ferdinand "was murdered by a Bosnian student, but there has never been any doubt that it was the instigation of the Austrian government that the deed was committed," Stephen Raymer, a prominent Yugoslav in the Vancouver community said. "But, further, they wanted an excuse to attack Serbia."

Austria-Hungary needed Serbia, Raymer said, to build a great railway on Serbian land.

The war also had an effect on civilians. It was an event, one member of the Canadian Club said, that caused Canada to find her soul.

"Canada! The magic name of the youngest of nations," the *Vancouver Daily World* said. "Canada, loved by the Motherland, honored beyond compare by the Allies, feared and hated by the Hun, and risen, in four short years, from a struggling colony to a mighty nation, called to the council board of powers..."

In the United States, several government agencies were working together to make Nov. 11 a national holiday. The agencies weren't alone. Armistice Day, the papers speculated, would become an international holiday.

A Time to Die

The end of the war came at time when both the United States and Canada needed a cause for celebration. For months, a global influenza pandemic had been raging. It was nicknamed the Spanish Flu because Spain, a neutral country during the war and thus free from wartime censorship, reported freely on the illness. The flu came in waves, each more deadly than the previous. Unlike the seasonal influenza people recognized, Spanish Flu killed young, healthy adults. The primary cause of death, however, was respiratory complications, and victims drowned to death from fluid filled lungs.

The sickness began in March, perhaps earlier. As the pandemic grew worse, government officials put towns and cities on quarantine. Any large gathering was banned. Churches, schools, dance halls, libraries, cinemas and businesses closed while social organizations cancelled meetings. In some areas, food distribution stations were established.

People were advised how to behave:

- Stay away from the sick
- Keep your home ventilated
- Get enough sleep
- Wear a gauze mask
- Eat a wholesome diet
- Turn your head so as not to inhale air someone else recently exhaled

In October, the sickness and illness rates rose dramatically, and Chicago called a meeting to discuss what could be done to curb the virus' spread. Throughout Illinois, 200 communities had a sharp increase in new cases while in the small town of Stronghurst, its two physicians were dead.

Oakland, California, Commissioner of Public Health and Safety Fred Morris ordered the police to arrest anyone not wearing a gauze mask. The move was backed by the city government and came in response to people largely ignoring the mayor's recommendation to wear masks.

At the University of California, Berkley, the 1,400 men enrolled in the Student Army Training Corps were kicked out of their barracks. University officials felt this would curb the spread of the disease, and the students were moved to tents.

U.S. Surgeon-General Rupert Blue released a statement, hoping to qualm the public's fears. The statement included this information:

- The illness usually disappears after three or four days unless pneumonia or meningitis sets in
- Fevers sometimes rise as high as 104 degrees
- The germ which causes the flu [referred to by Blue erroneously as bacteria] is spread person to person via small mucus droplets
- Ill persons are to stay home and rest
- Becoming ill with influenza does not cause lifetime immunity
- Keep out of crowds as much as possible and alleviate overcrowding at home
- "Cover up each cough and sneeze. If you don't, you'll spread the disease."
- Caregivers at home must take care not to spread the illness to others in the household

Blue advised caregivers to cover their clothing and wear a mask when entering the sickroom and to remove the garments immediately after. Caregiver instructions also were printed in the *Winnipeg Tribune*. They included not annoying the patient by fussing too much, keeping the patient's mouth clean with mouthwash, and combing the patient's hair.

Fresh air was thought to defeat the spread of the flu, so in Washington, D.C., all public transportation vehicles were required to operate with the windows open, no matter the weather. The health department's slogan was "GET THE AIR!" The public transportation order came after death rates in the city rose from 4.4 deaths per 1,000 people in early October to 32.4 deaths per 1,000 people a week later. For comparison, in 2016 the death rate in the United States was eight per 1,000 people, according to United Nations data, and 844 per 100,000, according to the Centers for Disease Control.

"Of the total number of influenza cases, the death rate is 6 percent," the *Chicago Tribune* reported, "and of the total pneumonia cases 34.3 percent."

The situation in Oakland was more severe. There, the death rate was as high as 25 percent at some hospitals.

Other deaths, like that of Steve Duboda in Belvidere, Illinois, were blamed on flu madness. Duboda leapt to his death from his hospital window. In Oakland, Lugo Franceschini tried to slash his own throat. He was described as delirious from the flu.

The situation overwhelmed hospitals, and medical personnel often were among the victims. Countless hospitals sought volunteer nurses and ambulance drivers.

In Winnipeg, the situation had "assumed alarming proportions." The city's health officer, A. J. Douglas, urged people to avoid crowds and get inoculated with anti-pneumonia serum.

"In the last 24 hours, 285 new cases were recorded," the *Winnipeg Tribune* said on Oct. 29. "Of these, 183 have been reported since midnight. Six additional deaths occurred, bringing the deaths from the 1,401 cases announced during the maladay [sic] to a total of 40."

More than 1,000 people were being treated in Winnipeg hospitals while only 240 had been released.

On the weekend of Nov. 2 and 3, there were 799 new cases and 35 deaths, but there also was cause for optimism. "Recoveries offset the number of new cases," the *Tribune* said, "indicating to the authorities that more control over the epidemic is being obtained."

For months, newspaper reports chronicled prominent citizens who died. They included soldiers, businessmen and educators. People across every socio-economic strata were affected, although some regions, and even some city neighborhoods, were hit harder than others.

The Desperate and the Dubious

For the most part, the public had very credible medical information, but this didn't stop wild theories. George Corsan, a YMCA swimming specialist, said people don't die of the flu because the flu produces a high fever and anyone strong enough to have their body produce a strong fever can recover from one. Instead, he blamed the caregivers. People who have a fever should not be fed, he said, because digestion stops during a fever. The patients either die from constipation or from colon slime being forced into the lungs. The slime, Corsan said, is called pneumonia.

"All food is a poison during fever," Corsan said, "and the idea of feeding a fever patient to keep up his strength is the cause of deaths from the present plague. Also, I feel sure that smallpox deaths are the result of constipation and not skin eruptions."

Corsan said whiskey decreased the power of the liver, the organ he felt was responsible for immunity, and that salt deprived the blood of serum.

His suggestions for keeping well? Take five enemas before bed, each one increasingly stronger; drink plenty of water or fruit juice; open the windows because hot air causes lung weakness; and at the first sign of a fever, which Corsan said could reach 140 degrees, take a hot bath. It is unknown whether the 140 degrees was a contemporary typo that should have read 104 or whether Corsan actually believed this.

The root of the problem, Corsan said, is that the United States is overfed. People should eat fruits, vegetables and grains, he said, and limit dairy and meat.

As it was a mystery why some people survived from the flu and others did not, "cures" often were attributed to a person's recovery. A Winnipeg resident named Robert Snook said he was cured by hot drinks and hot water bottles at his feet.

The faithful would be free of disease if they remained fearless, churches said. Fear makes the body susceptible to illness, they believed.

A TALE OF TWO NATIONS: CANADA, U.S. AND WWI

"There is no question that by the right attitude of mind these people have kept themselves from illness," Iowa physician Dr. Witte said. "I have no doubt that many persons have contracted the disease through fear. People can deceive themselves into thinking they have any disease [in the book], and doubtless many have thought themselves into their graves."

Christian Scientists, especially, seemed to have a cure for the flu that other religious groups did not. "Adherents of this faith here have undoubtedly enjoyed immunity from contagion to a remarkable degree," the *Vancouver Daily World* said, "while those who have resorted to it for relief from influenza state that their recovery has been rapid."

The unscrupulous also began to take advantage of the situation. In Santa Monica, landlords advertised their seaside apartments as being contagion-free and the ideal way to beat the epidemic.

Even more unscrupulous were the merchants who hocked products to a desperate public. Multiple drug advertisements appeared in a typical newspaper edition. Here are some examples:

An advertisement for Kennedy's Tonic Port disguised itself as a legitimate article. Only the "adv." in the lower right corner gave it away. The advertisement ran in Canada with the headline "Why so large a death rate in Canada and no deaths in South American from influenza?"

The "article" claimed there had been no influenza deaths in South America and attributed this to the local practice of seeping Cinchona tree bark in wine. Little did people know, it said, that this is exactly what Kennedy's Tonic Port was. Every household should have a bottle, it said, as it cured not only influenza but anemia, women's diseases, coughs, colds, bronchitis and asthma.

Another product was Horlick's Malted Milk. It claimed to be "The diet during and after influenza," being a real food-drink endorsed by physicians.

Milburn's Heart and Nerve Pills guaranteed to restore a person to health as he recovered from influenza.

"This terrible scourge leaves in its wake weak hearts, shattered nerves, impoverished blood, and a general run-down debilitated condition on the system," the ad said.

Crisis Passing?

Oakland's flu statistics, published in the Oakland Tribune on Nov. 8, illustrate how the flu progressed that autumn in many communities in North America. On Oct. 2, there was one new case and no deaths. This figure spiked to a high of 578 new cases on Oct. 24. Deaths reached their peak a few days later, Nov. 1, at 39. When the *Tribune* went to press on Nov. 8, there were only 11 new cases, but 472 people had died since Oct. 1.

Manitoba's rural areas were seeing a decrease in new cases. *Only* 162 new cases were reported in a three-day period in early November. The following weekend, it dropped to 114 new cases. City officials in Winnipeg also were beginning to think the crisis had passed. On the afternoon of Nov. 11, there were 80 new cases and 18 deaths.

In Vancouver, public officials planned to meet Nov. 12 to discuss lifting the ban on public gatherings. The number of discharges was outnumbering the number of admissions at the city's four hospitals, and the number of new cases and deaths had fallen as well, according to the health department.

On Armistice Day, a number of other communities also were considering lifting the band.

The pandemic killed more people globally than the war, the *Brooklyn Daily Eagle* reported on Dec. 21, and the U.S. government was forced to pay $170 million in life insurance for soldiers who died of the flu.

Between Sept. 15 and Dec. 5 alone, U.S. public health officials estimated between 300,000 and 350,000 Americans died. This compared to 58,478 military deaths during the war. It also was greater than the total American war casualties which were 262,693.

• • • •

By the time it was over, the Great War had killed more than 35 million people. Of those, 61,000 were Canadian and 126,000 were American.

Influenza took an additional 20 million to 100 million people including an estimated 675,000 Americans and as many as 50,000 Canadians

Glossary

Americanism: An ideology aimed at creating an American identity

Continent: Mainland Europe

Hyphenism: Hyphenating one's nationality. Example, German-American.

Kills: The number of enemy aircraft a pilot shot down.

No Man's Land: The land between two opposing army's trenches or front lines.

Penny Dreadful: Cheap, mass produced pop fiction novels in the late 19th and early 20th centuries.

Plank: A declaration of a candidate's opinions, plans or goals.

Platform: A political party's policies, values and beliefs.

Progressive Party: A faction of the Republican Party founded by former President Teddy Roosevelt in 1912. Also known as the Bull Moose Party.

Rooseveltians: Teddy Roosevelt's supporters during the 1916 election season

Salient: An outward projection in a battle line.

Suffragist: A person advocating for the right to vote, especially for women. This compares to a suffragette who used organized and sometimes violent civil protest to achieve the same goal.

Sources

The information in *A Tale of Two Nations* came exclusively from articles in the following newspapers and websites.

Belvidere Daily Republican:

December 6, 1918

Brooklyn Daily Eagle:

December 21, 1918

The Chicago Tribune:

June 28, 1914; July 29, 1914; July 30, 1914; July 31, 1914; Aug. 1, 1914; Aug. 2, 1914; May 8, 1915; May 9, 1915; May 10, 1915; May 12, 1915; May 14, 1915; May 15, 1915; May 17, 1915; May 18, 1915; June 7, 1916; June 8, 1916; June 9, 1916; June 10, 1916; April 1, 1917; April 2, 1917; April 3, 1917; April 4, 1917; April 5, 1917; April 6, 1917; April 7, 1917; October 9, 1918; October 21, 1918; November 11, 1918; November 12, 1918

The Los Angeles Daily News:

July 28, 1914; July 29, 1914; July 30, 1914; July 31, 1914; Aug. 1, 1914; Aug. 2, 1914; Aug. 3, 1914; Aug. 4, 1914; May 7, 1915; May 8, 1915; May 9, 1915; May 11, 1915; May 12, 1915; May 13, 1915; May 14, 1915; April 1, 1917; April 2, 1917; April 3, 1917; April 5, 1917; April 7, 1917; October 13, 1918; October 25, 1918

The Manitoba Free Press:
April 23, 1915; April 26, 1915; April 27, 1915; April 28, 1915; April 30, 1915

Mattoon Journal Gazette:

December 5, 1918

The New York Evening World:
May 1, 1915
The New York Times:

June 28, 1914; July 29, 1914; July 30, 1914; July 31, 1914; Aug. 1, 1914; Aug. 2, 1914; April 20, 1915; May 8, 1915; May 9, 1915; May 10, 1915; May 11, 1915; May 12, 1915; May 13, 1915; May 14, 1915; May 15, 1915; May 16, 1915; May 17, 1915; April 1, 1917; April 2, 1917; April 3, 1917; April 4, 1917; April 5, 1917; April 6, 1917; April 7, 1917; November 11, 1918; November 12, 1918

Nanaimo Daily News:

April 10, 1917

Oakland Tribune:

October 24, 1918; October 31, 1918; November 8, 1918

The Ottawa Journal:

Aug. 4, 1914; Aug. 5 1914; April 22, 1915; April 24, 1915; April 26, 1915; April 27, 1915; April 28, 1915; April 29, 1915; April 30, 1915; September 16, 1916; September 18, 1916; September 19, 1916; September 21, 1916; April 9, 1917; April 10, 1917; April 11, 1917; April 12, 1917; April 13, 1917; November 11, 1918

St. Louis Post Dispatch:

June 14, 1916; June 15, 1916

St. Louis Star and Times:

June 14, 1916; June 17, 1916

Vancouver Daily World:

Aug. 1, 1914; Aug. 2, 1914; Aug. 3, 1914; Aug. 4, 1914; April 22, 1915; April 23, 1915; April 24, 1915; April 26, 1915; April 27, 1915; April 28, 1915; April 29, 1915; April 30, 1915; May 1, 1915; May 3, 1915; August 2, 1916; September 16, 1916; September 18, 1916; September 19, 1916; September 20, 1916; September 21, 1916; November 11, 1918

The Washington Post:

November 7, 1916; November 8, 1916; November 9, 1916; November 11, 1916

The Winnipeg Tribune:

June 28, 1914; June 29, 1914; July 28, 1914; July 29, 1914; July 30, 1914; July 31, 1914; Aug. 3, 1914; July 1, 1916; September 18, 1916; September 22, 1916; September 23, 1916; April 10, 1917; April 11, 1917; April 12, 1917; October 12, 1918; October 29, 1918; November 4, 1918; November 11, 1918; November 12, 1918; November 25, 1918

The Canadian Encyclopedia

http://www.thecanadianencyclopedia.ca/en/article/first-world-war-wwi/

http://www.thecanadianencyclopedia.ca/en/article/influenza/

CBC News

http://www.cbc.ca/news/canada/newfoundland-labrador/beaumont-hamel-what-went-wrong-1.3654924

http://www.cbc.ca/news/canada/newfoundland-labrador/beaumont-hamel-soldiers-victims-not-heroes-died-for-nothing-1.3656510

Centers for Disease Control and Prevention

https://www.cdc.gov/nchs/fastats/deaths.htm

History
https://www.history.com/topics/1918-flu-pandemic

• • • •

History Wiz
http://www.historywiz.com/lusitanianote.htm
World Bank
https://data.worldbank.org/indicator/SP.DYN.CDRT.IN
WW1 Facts
http://ww1facts.net/quick-reference/ww1-casualties/

Don't miss out!

Visit the website below and you can sign up to receive emails whenever Melina Druga publishes a new book. There's no charge and no obligation.

https://books2read.com/r/B-A-YBDN-QOWLB

BOOKS 2 READ

Connecting independent readers to independent writers.

Also by Melina Druga

A Tale of Two Nations
1914
1915
1916
1917
1918
A Tale of Two Nations: Canada, U.S. and WWI

Enterprising Women
Enterprising Women: A Practical Guide to Starting Your First Business
Enterprising Women: Practical Advice for First Time Entrepreneurs

The Rock Star's Wife
Sexual Awakening

WWI Trilogy
Angel of Mercy
Those Left Behind
Adjustment Year

Standalone
Heinous: Forgotten Murders From the 1910s
Journey of Hope
Rose's Assignment
The Unmarriable Kind

Watch for more at www.melinadruga.com.

About the Author

Melina Druga is a freelance journalist, history enthusiast and author. Her focus is on the period 1890-1920 with a particular interest in WWI and how the war changed the lives of ordinary people.

Based in the Midwest, Melina lives with her husband, daughter and cat.

Follow Melina on social media @MelinaDruga.

For more information, visit www.melinadruga.com.

Read more at www.melinadruga.com.

About the Publisher

Sun Up Press publishes both fiction and nonfiction titles.

Printed in the USA
CPSIA information can be obtained
at www.ICGtesting.com
LVHW011511311223
767823LV00049B/1912